I want you to succeed!

Best Wishes, Professor Bernie

SOME REAL-LIFE STUDENT STORIES (The Problem)

- Many students don't know how to study-and the results are panic, fear, anger, low self-esteem and a sense of betrayal
- Students break down in tears in my office, frustrated because they don't know how to study and are only scraping by
- Students swear at me in front of the class when they fail an assignment and say it's my fault they failed-they feel betrayed by the system
- Some students openly cheat by copying from the Internet and don't see this as an ethical problem
- On a radio talk show where I was a guest, a mother speaks about her son who is going through therapy because his teacher ridiculed him for failing
- A student submits an assignment full of the details of his sexual exploits over the summer and can't see why he got an F
- A student's marriage broke up because his weak study skills forced him to drop out of college

SOME TIPS FROM "THE PROFESSOR'S SECRETS" TO HELP YOU SUCCEED (The Solution)

- *Take notes from your notes.* Take a few minutes each day to highlight key points from your lecture notes onto an index card. Gather these cards for each course and review them at the end of each week. What you'll gradually develop is a "profile" of highlights to create a structure for each course.

- *Practice "reverse procrastination."* List whatever prevents you from getting to your studies now-going to a movie, sitting at an outdoor patio-and treat them instead as your later bonus for getting at your work now. By doing this, you're reversing their status from "impediment" to studying to "reward" for studying.

- *Don't skip classes or miss assignments.* I never hear about as many scourges of family deaths, plagues of personal illness, and calamities involving technological breakdowns as I do at "assignment time." And the excuses are so creative: "My grandmother has SLOWLY been dying"; "I've had a lot of appointments with my parole officer"; "I had to leave the country unexpectedly"; "My money ran out so I had to get a full-time job for the past two months"; "My daycare vanished so I had to stay home with my kids"; "My car was stolen so I had to look for it"; "My wife is pregnant so I had to stay home"; "I'm cutting a CD with my band and lost track of time." Don't spend your time thinking of excuses instead of doing your work.

- *Take your watch off and put it in front of you.* Use this as a visual reminder to divide your time among the test questions. When you actually see your watch in front of you (even if there's a clock in the room), you'll be prompted to pay more attention to using your time well.

- *Know the difference between "compare" and "contrast."* When students confuse test directions they won't get the top marks—so know how to follow instructions clearly. For example, when you compare two ideas, techniques, or concepts, you're showing how they're alike in terms of their similarities or differences. Contrasting two or more ideas, techniques, or concepts means that you show only how they're different from each other.

- *Recycle your effort.* If you've done well on a test, "recycle" that effort by using it to help yourself on an upcoming test or exam. For example, if you know that the test you just wrote covered certain chapters that will also appear on the mid-term exam, you can use what you learned from the test when you write the exam. This will save you considerable effort at a later date.

- *Don't cheat – whose work are you copying from anyway?* Students who cheat are making one huge, false assumption: that the student they're copying from actually knows what the right answers are! What do they know about this person? Do they know if that student is prepared, has studied, or has even read the book? And what if that student is guessing? What they're doing is actually putting the outcome for their own success in the hands of a complete stranger, and all this really does is expose their own level of desperation.

- *Use the "game show" strategy with your study group.* Take turns playing the "host" who makes up short, factual questions about dates, places, people, inventions and so on. Choose either a random or ordered selection of "contestants" from the group who try to get the right answer. You can even have "prizes" of snacks, fruit or nuts, or pretend "bonus test marks" to give out for the correct answer.

PLUS... LEARN ABOUT OTHER HELPFUL HINTS

- *"8 Great Ways To Student Success"*
- *The 15-Minute Rule*
- *The Lurching Express*
- *"Energy Vampires"*
- *A "Great Books" Reading List*
- *Definitions of Test Terms*
- *Sample Test Questions*

THE PROFESSOR'S SECRETS:
BREAKING THE SILENCE-
HOW TO GET TOP MARKS ON TESTS AND EXAMS

Canadian Cataloguing in Publication Data
Gaidosch, Bernie
    The Professor's Secrets:
    Breaking The Silence-How To Get Top Marks On Tests And Exams

ISBN   0-9730335-1-7

Published by: Daimon Corp. and Classic Legal Publications Inc.

This book is dedicated to
all students with the desire and motivation
to move ahead and succeed

CONTENTS

PART 1

Why You Need This Book 1
How To Use This Book 2
My Thanks Go To 3
Some Real-Life Student Stories 3

PART 2

Why Do You Need To Learn How To Study? 19
Why Good Students Are Like Good Athletes 20
Where Do These Techniques Come From? 21
Do You Feel Motivated To Improve? 24
Some Tips To Help Boost Your Motivation 27
Motivation Is The Springboard To Success 30

PART 3

What Approach Should You Take To Studying? 35
You Decide 37
The First Step — Long-Term Study Strategies 38
"Plan The Work—Then Work The Plan" 39
Think Of A Soaring Eagle Looking Down 39
Take Stock Of Each Semester 40
Judge The Degree Of Difficulty Among Semesters 41
How To Prepare For A Semester 42
How To Spend Your Time In A Semester 43
The Benefits Of Our Long-Term Approach 44

PART 4

Medium-Term Study Strategies 49
The Value Of Lectures 50
Taking Good Notes 51
Where Do You Do Your Best Studying? 55
How Do You Manage Study Time? 57
Should You Use A Study Group? 60

PART 5

Short-Term Study Strategies 67
Assess Your Needs 68
What Kind Of Learner Are You? 68
Do You Have A Study System? 71
How Do You Deal With Test Stress? 75
Do You Tend To Procrastinate? 77
Do You Have A Preparation Checklist? 81

Part 6

How Your Professor Sees You 87
What Not To Do In Class 88
How To Deal With Your Professors 93
Whose Courses Are They Anyway? 98

Part 7

Why Write Tests? 105
The Difference Between Tests And Exams 106
What To Do Before A Test... 107
What To Do During A Test 109
What To Do After A Test 112

Part 8

Where To Get Help With Study Techniques 119
The Bell Curve And What It Means To You 121
Appealing Your Grade.. 122
Why Not Cheat? 123
Studying For Online Courses 125

Part 9

Can Students' Appearance Affect Their Marks? 131
What If You Don't Like Your Professor? 132
The 8 Great Ways To Student Success 133
A "Great Books" Reading List 137
A Few Bonus Tips 138
Thoughts To Remember... 140

Part 10

Test Terms 145
Sample Test Questions 147

PART 1

WHY YOU NEED THIS BOOK

The need for this book has become apparent to me over my many years as a professor. During this time, I've watched as many students struggled with writing tests and exams and tried to get the best marks possible. I'd do everything I could to help them, but all too often they would fail or, at best, scrape by with low marks.

For the most part, these were "good" or "above average" students, people who had the ability to do well, but who were missing the study techniques or the "shortcuts" to get the top marks. They had the best intentions of doing a top-notch job in their studies, and they were motivated because many had made sacrifices to continue their academic careers in college or university. The problem was that each of them had to "reinvent the wheel," learning firsthand and on their own what should have been available to all of them to get the job done well and quickly.

It's much like learning how to swim. You can jump into the water on your own and try to figure it out, but why not get some coaching to learn the basics and then to progress from there? Why waste time and effort learning what others already know, when instead you can use their knowledge to make it easier for yourself?

That's why I needed to write this book. I'm like the coach who's sharing my techniques and tips learned over all these years so that your job as a student can be easier.

I'm giving my " professor's secrets" so that you can achieve as much as possible, as easily as possible, and as quickly as possible. I want to give you the secrets of getting good marks and show you what your teachers and professors are really looking for.

You can then use what you need to know to become a better student and get the top marks on tests and exams. As we know, top marks are still the "currency" of education, and the "richest" students know the techniques to get them.

HOW TO USE THIS BOOK

I've set up this book so you can use it in one of two ways.

First, you can go through it from beginning to end, reading the sections in the order in which they appear to get a full sense of the many things you can do to make yourself a better student. This approach works well if you have the time.

The other approach you can take is to read it in segments as needed. If you have a test or exam coming up and need some help with what to do in the actual test room, just focus on that section of the book to deal with that immediate situation. Later, you can go back to other sections on an "as needed" basis, or find the time to get through the whole book when appropriate.

This is the same approach I advise students to use in my book on essay writing—*The Professor's Secrets: Breaking The Silence—How To Write Essays And Term Papers*. Most people will judge what their needs are and weigh them against their time constraints to make the right choice.

I've also kept the book short and to the point—I believe that "learning how to learn" should be as clear and direct as possible. Students shouldn't have to spend more of their precious time on study strategies and test writing techniques than they do on what it is they're in school to learn.

One practical suggestion: to get the most out of this book, don't be reluctant to mark it up with markers, highlighters, and post-its for quick and easy reference. Identify and capture the shortcuts to the learning process to get top marks.

While throughout the book I refer to "professors" rather than to "teachers," this is by no means meant to exclude anyone who works as a teacher or an instructor. My teaching environment happens to be in a post-secondary institution so it's natural for me to refer to that context. However, everything I write about here can be just as usefully applied in junior high or high school as well.

MY THANKS GO TO...

There are usually special people to acknowledge for what often seems to be only one person's effort.

And that is certainly the case here. For her inspiration and unfailing support—and her ongoing love—I thank my wife, Maureen.

My appreciation also goes to my friend, Ken Dickson, for his thoughtful suggestions; to the irrepressibly caring Spider Jones for his enthusiasm and concern; and to my long-time friend, Gregory Byrne, for sharing his insights as a writer of student life.

I also thank my parents, Irma and Larry, for their love and support over the years.

Finally, I want to sincerely acknowledge my dear friend, Norman Stachiw, who passed away far too soon in 2001. Norm was a fine teacher who spent his life helping students.

SOME REAL-LIFE STUDENT STORIES

Students can start out with the grandest of hopes and plans for their studies, but in the end, never achieve them.

Many students can imagine the successes they might attain in high school, college or university—such things as top marks, the Dean's Honor Roll, or the beginnings of career success. But too many end up only ever imagining these things because they remain elusive—they end up scraping through their academic careers with marks of C or D, or they fail or drop out. For them, the "good things" are always something that's in their imagination or an image of "what might have been."

They come through their educational experience, look back, and think "Well, it didn't go nearly as well as I wanted it to, but somehow I got through it, and it's over with."

What's important for you to know, however, is that it doesn't have to be this way. But, it's also important to know that for too many students this is the only way it ever is.

That's why I begin this book with stories of students who had some sad and terrible experiences. My hope is that readers, both students and parents, will learn something from what these people went through. My hope is also that, if you are a student, you can use your understanding of these situations to keep from going through them yourself.

And, while I've changed their names, their situations are indeed real—all of these students found themselves struggling and frustrated only because they didn't have the writing and study skills necessary to do well.

Laura was a third-year university student majoring in History. One day she came to see me about an important final essay she'd written and asked for my advice. I read the beginning and ending of the paper and asked her to describe for me in her own words what the essay was about.

She looked down and said, "I don't know," and then started to cry. When she stopped crying, I told her I didn't mean to upset her. I was simply asking her to tell me about her essay—it was a perfectly appropriate and reasonable question.

She replied that she wasn't upset about the question, but rather about the fact that she couldn't answer it!

It turned out that, even though she was in university for three years, she really didn't know what she was doing when it came to writing an essay. She admitted that she was "faking it" all this time. Her approach to an essay was to load words related to the topic onto pages. She had no idea what her professors wanted her to do in their writing assignments.

She was getting marks of C's and D's for all this time. I couldn't help but feel that the tears she cried that day were the release of an incredible amount of frustration and despair.

Jason was a student of mine in a General Education class in college. When I returned his mid-term exam and he saw that he got an F, he turned to me and started swearing at me in front of the whole class.

He called me several "dirty names" and said that it was my fault for giving him a failing grade! He said that he couldn't be blamed for something that he didn't know and that he was never taught.

When I asked him what he meant, he said that he'd never been taught how to study in high school and that he certainly wasn't taught how to study in college. He couldn't see how it was possibly fair for me to fail him for something he never knew how to do in the first place!

He later apologized for his behavior, but said that he felt betrayed and hurt for getting this far along in the school system and still not knowing what he needed to know in order to succeed.

Lam was a student in an English as Second Language class a number of years ago. He tried very hard to do his best to succeed, but couldn't do much better than marks of F or D.

He was clearly frustrated by what he saw to be his genuine efforts that only ever brought the same lack of results. One day, when he got back another assignment with yet another failing grade, it seemed almost too much for him. Fighting back tears, he came to me after the class was over and said "Sir, I'll never be like you because I cannot even speak English good enough, never mind even writing like you!"

I waited till he calmed down, and then told him "But Lam, in a way you are like me." I went on to explain that my parents had also been immigrants and that when I arrived with them I couldn't speak English either. Like Lam, I had to go through the struggles of learning to speak, read and write the language, but I'd persevered and had overcome the obstacles.

Lam couldn't believe his ears when he heard this—I guess that to him I seemed so far removed from any idea of what was attainable that he just couldn't conceive of the two of us being on anything like the same level in terms of language and writing ability.

But the next time I saw him, he seemed different. It was as though he took in what I told him in a calm and believing way. He set about his work with a quiet determination, and, from week to week, started to show small improvements in his writing. By the end of the semester, while he wasn't making vast strides in his writing, he did stop failing. This, in itself, was a significant step in his progress—and it was just the kind of improvement he had to make before he could take his work to the next level.

When I saw him in later semesters, he always had a warm smile and a vigorous handshake. He told me that he remembered what I said that day, and that he kept those words in his memory to help him whenever he struggled to overcome any difficulties in his life.

Lam was able to come to terms with his challenges because he could now understand that others—sometimes those whom he would least suspect—had been able to do what he was trying to achieve. It turned out that my seemingly unremarkable contact with Lam's experience turned out to be one of the most remarkable rewards in my career as a writing skills professor.

Gina was in a Media Studies course I once taught. One particular assignment called for students to research coverage of a given media event at that time and to provide an analysis of the material.

As a precaution to ensure that all of the work these students handed in was actually their own, I checked out the websites that related to that event (providing either current or historical information) and downloaded the most important ones to act as references.

When the assignments came in and I read Gina's, I was surprised to see that she had downloaded much of the same material as I had and then went on to do a "cut and paste" version, calling it her own work. Of course, I gave her assignment an F and returned it to her.

When she saw the F, she got angry with me and asked me what I thought I was doing by failing her.

When I explained that she failed the assignment because she plagiarized her essay, she almost couldn't believe what she was hearing. "How DARE you fail me for this," she said, "when all I'm doing is taking other people's information and summarizing it?"

"And, besides," she went on, "that's all information that's on the Internet, so naturally it's out there for anyone to use!"

I explained that she was hardly "summarizing" anything when she

6

used other writers' sentences and ideas as though they were her own. And, just because these articles were available on the Internet didn't mean that they were there for anyone to pick and use as though that was their own work. The simple fact that this information existed in what we call the "public domain" didn't make it "fair game" for students to call theirs—they still had to acknowledge it as a source for their own analysis.

In the end, Gina admitted that she'd done this before—in fact, she did it this way all the time she was in high school. She didn't think it was wrong to do it then, and she didn't think it was wrong now—that's why she was stunned when I failed her on this assignment. "I didn't do anything wrong," she said.

How did this happen? I wondered. How did Gina get through high school without a clear sense about right and wrong, between acceptable and unacceptable behavior when it came to passing off the work of others as her own?

She certainly put herself in a vulnerable position now, when her writing had to be her own, original work. She set herself up to fail in most of her courses—and what would happen to her later in the work world when she got a job? What would happen to her then if all she did was to copy and cheat?

Paul was a student in my Writing Skills class who did fairly good work in his in-class writing assignments, but did extremely well in his take-home assignments.

I was very pleased with his overall high level of work and I was very proud of him when he graduated and got a job. About a year after he left college, he knocked on my office door. I was happy to see him again and was looking forward to hearing how things were going for him at work. Of course, I expected to hear good things because he had been very much a "star" student.

Well, I certainly didn't expect to hear him say what he said that day, and, by the time he finished, I almost fell out of my chair!

"I have a confession to make, sir," he began. "I cheated my way through your classes—and most of my other ones—when I was in school, and I thought I was just being smart. When you talked about how important writing and studying were, when you said that would help me in my job, I thought that was just some goofball stuff you were saying!"

He went on to say that things were not going very well for him at the job he'd been at for the past six months (this was his second job since graduating). It was a good job as a sales rep at a wholesale clothing company, he said, and there was plenty of opportunity for advancement into promotions and marketing. He really liked the people he worked with and they liked him.

"The real problem," he said, " is that my job demands that I'm a kind of 'jack-of-all-trades' in the sense that I have to write sales letters, promotional pieces, memos, reports, summaries, and sometimes even the minutes of meetings! In other words, all the kinds of things I cheated on in school just to get through—and now I can't do them when I have to for my job!"

"I should have listened to what you said about needing to write for the work world a lot more seriously back then," he said. "I see now that you were right—and now I'm stuck because I can't really do the things I need to in order to do well at my job, or to get the promotion and raises I want."

Paul ended up going to night school for some courses as a "solution" to what he missed, but he knew it didn't have to be that way if he only understood the value of what we were learning in class the first time round.

Todd is someone I've never met, but I heard about him when I was a guest on a radio talk show, discussing students' struggles in school and my *Professor's Secrets* books. His mother phoned in toward the end of the program and began talking about her son's negative experience in high school.

She said that Todd was not a strong student, that he never had the study skills or writing ability he needed to get the top marks, and that over the years he was often made fun of by his classmates who called him "dummy" and "loser." Todd's self-esteem was already low and got even lower when one day his Grade 10 English teacher gave him back his latest assignment. Todd failed his book summary assignment, and when his teacher gave it back to him, he said, "You'll never amount to anything if you can't write a simple essay."

For Todd, this was the "last straw," his mother said. This remark from his teacher was one more insult piled on top of all the others that Todd had to endure over the years. He took this criticism particularly hard because he'd been working diligently to improve. Since these remarks came from his teacher, the person he was most trying to please and impress, Todd felt hurt and depressed. According to his mother, Todd developed feelings of worthlessness and wanted to quit school.

As it turned out, Todd went for counseling and therapy because his self-esteem had been beaten down so much.

Shella's parents came to my office quite upset about the fact that she dropped out of college. They couldn't understand it. She was such a diligent worker, they said. She was always up late at night working on her computer.

They were agitated and raised their voices so loudly that I had to get up to close the door. I didn't want the people in the hall to hear them screaming. After they finally calmed down and apologized for their behavior, we discussed Shella's situation.

I explained to them that Shella was scraping by with marks of D's and low C's in all of her courses. I also told them that I failed her for handing in an assignment that was completely copied from someone else. That "someone else," it turned out, was her older sister, Mila.

Mila had been a student in my writing class. While in my class, she submitted an excellent essay on "The History and Development of Aboriginal Rights." This was a thoughtful and well-written analysis of the topic. She received an A+ on the paper. As a matter of fact, I kept a copy as an example of a superior essay to use as a model for students in other classes.

I asked Shella's parents to imagine my surprise when Shella handed in the same paper that her sister submitted two years before, claiming it to be her own original work.

When I confronted her, she broke down in tears and admitted she'd attempted to pass off her sister's paper as her own—but only as a last resort to try to boost her marks so that she could stay in her program. When that didn't work, she just dropped out because "she couldn't take it any more." The stress and pressure of "trying to keep her head above the pass line" became too much for her and she just walked away from it.

When her parents found out, they became upset because they couldn't put together their impression of her as an "average" student with what she had done. What they didn't know was that she wasn't even an average student—what they found out was that she had some serious deficiencies in her skills as a student and that these led her to desperate measures.

Goran was a likeable student who worked hard to learn English. He had a great sense of humor and was always learning and passing around "English jokes." He was a favorite in the class and the rest of the students appreciated his outgoing nature and liked the fact that his attempts to learn the language didn't prevent him from having fun and sticking his linguistic neck out with his funny "yokes," as he used to call them.

It was around the fourth week of class in the fall semester when I gave out the essay topic choices, one of which was the perennial favorite, "What I Did On My Summer Vacation." I always put a few of the "fun" topics into this batch so that students would "loosen up" as writers right from the start of the course.

What I didn't suspect was that, for Goran, "flexible" and "loose" were simply operative terms. When I read his essay on the "summer vacation" topic, I was completely bowled over.

He wrote a sufficiently clear and well-expressed essay, all right—in fact, it read quite well in terms of having a clear thesis statement, well-chosen and detailed examples for support, and a rousing conclusion that left a clear sense of focus and direction in my mind. Well done, Goran! He even minimized the grammar, sentence structure, and spelling mistakes.

The only problem with it, however, was his use of the topic—because Goran had met and slept with a number of young women over that summer, he made his topic "The Sexual Exploits of My Summer Vacation."

He obviously put a lot of thought and effort into the writing of this provocative topic, and on the merit of structure and writing alone I would have to give it a good mark, a B+ or an A-. He must have felt the same way because he was caught completely off guard when I gave it back to him with an F.

When he came to my office howling with surprise and outrage, he said he couldn't believe I failed him on this "good" essay. He wanted to know why!

I explained to him that the writing itself was quite good and deserved a high mark, but that his topic choice was entirely unacceptable as content for post-secondary courses. This was not an appropriate forum for the minute details of his sexual "conquests," no matter how well written they were.

He said it was all in "good humor" and that he didn't intend any harm by writing about this. I told him that there were obviously limits as to what is perceived as humor in the context of our learning environment and that he'd crossed the line this time.

He still couldn't see the validity of what I was saying and finally just shrugged and walked away. But he talked to me about this situation later that semester and agreed that he should have understood what was right to do from the start.

Where I usually struggle to get students to see that "how you say it" is as important as "what you say," in this case it was the reverse. I had to work hard to get Goran to see that the "what" part is at least as meaningful as the "how."

Bill and **Farah** were a young couple in their 20s who were married for about two years when they decided that Bill should enroll in a marketing program at college to improve their prospects for the future.

In his first semester, a pattern started to unfold. Bill was passing courses in Finance and Math, but was failing and barely passing in other courses that required more in the way of writing skills, analytical thinking, and creative study skills.

When Bill showed up in my Basic Writing Skills course, he was obviously struggling with poor language skills, particularly grammar and sentence structure. As well, when it came to writing exams, both mid-terms and finals, he had difficulty using his time effectively and understanding what the questions were asking him to do.

These difficulties continued in the following semester when he was also enrolled in my Business Writing class. He had trouble writing his information memos and persuasive letters—and, when it came to doing his business report, the result was more or less a disaster!

He worked hard enough to get through the course, though, and managed to just pass. Unfortunately, he was not able to pull off a pass in the next semester.

I ran into him a couple of times that term and asked how things were going. I had suggested several ways he could find extra help and was eager to see if he'd followed up with any of them. What he told me, though, caught me by surprise.

He said that, in addition to struggling to do his best in his courses, he was working part-time to support himself and his wife. The stress of trying to get through his courses was now doubled by the stress of working during his spare time rather than being able to do the necessary studying and homework. He said that, at this rate, he wasn't sure how much longer he could take the pressure.

I tried to stay in touch with him after that, but I didn't see him around campus that much. At a later point, I thought he might just show up at my office to see me, but that too didn't happen. It was only about a year later, when speaking to another professor about what became of certain students we both had in our classes, that I heard about Bill.

It seemed that he couldn't take it any more towards the end—that, because things were so bad for him in his courses, he ended up dropping out and returning to a part-time job he had as an office cleaner.

But there was also another consequence I heard about, one that made me even sadder—it turned out that Bill and his wife had separated.

When I heard this, I couldn't help but think that Bill's failed attempt at school also took its toll on his marriage. After all, his hope for success in college was the main reason he was there in the first place. Of course, there probably were other factors involved, but when I remembered the pressure he was under in school and his eventual failure at achieving his goals, I somehow knew that Bill's marriage was also a "victim" of what he failed to accomplish.

These stories demonstrate students' feelings of frustration, bitterness, resentment, low self-esteem and betrayal. They show the lives of these people in turmoil and how their learning inadequacies—real or perceived—can harm them to extreme degrees.

People all too often think that the consequences students suffer behind the "closed doors" of high school, college or university are only the academic ones of low marks or failing grades. What these stories show, however, is that there exists an ongoing "human and emotional impact" which is also part of the price students pay when they lack certain skills.

These are the consequences I've seen far too frequently over my many teaching years. And keeping them for happening—or at least attempting to diminish them—is what I want to do for students by writing this book.

NOTES

NOTES

NOTES

NOTES

NOTES

PART 2

WHY DO YOU NEED TO LEARN HOW TO STUDY?

I've often heard students say to me, "Why do I need to learn how to study? Isn't it obvious? Don't students just *know* how to study anyway?"

There is certainly a "right" and "wrong" or "true" and "false" aspect to these questions. That is, for the most part, there *are* obvious aspects to activities we refer to as studying.

Think about this for a moment. When students engage in such activities as taking notes, reading chapters before lectures, working in study groups, and cramming for tests and exams, we call these activities some form of studying.

But there is a difference between "studying" and how one goes about studying—and the difference lies in the technique of studying.

Knowing how to use certain study techniques makes all the difference in the world between those who achieve the top marks and those who just scrape by or fail.

WHY GOOD STUDENTS ARE LIKE GOOD ATHLETES

At the beginning of this book, I referred to my task of helping students as similar to that of a coach who teaches people how to swim.

It's helpful to think in terms of that same example now. When athletes—whether they are swimmers, runners, or skiers—set out to improve their skills, they have a basic skill or training level behind them already.

So, too, does a student—whether in high school, college, or university—have the basic learning and study skills that have been acquired over a number of years all the way from kindergarten and elementary school.

But this is where the similarity usually ends.

Athletes have already spent hours, days, weeks, and years getting to an "intermediate" or "advanced" level where, now, they're ready to work with a coach to take them to the highest plateau possible. They understand fully that, in order to get the maximum out of their abilities, in order to reach the "gold" podium, they have to keep on "learning how to learn."

They know, almost without having to say it, that they need their coach to teach them how to cut seconds and milliseconds off their times, how to build their endurance to a high level, and how to think in terms of their competitors so that they can gain an edge over those competitors.

But is this what students do? Do they even address the skills that will help them become better as students and get those top marks—or do they simply *assume* that they already have those skills because, after all, they ended up this far, didn't they?

If I were to ask any committed athlete—or, for that matter, musician, dancer, or actor—if they felt they absolutely needed to continue to learn how to refine their skills on an ongoing basis, I think it's fair to say that not only would the answer be "yes," but that it would be understood as a given.

So why isn't that the same with students? Why isn't it understood by students that, in order for them to achieve the most that they can—in order for them to get the top marks, scholarships, or meet their entrance requirements—they need to learn certain techniques in their area in the same way that athletes learn them in theirs.

Well, they do need to. And you need to. That's why I'm giving out my "coach's techniques," or rather my "professor's secrets," so that you can get it right and get it right quickly!

There's no reason at all that you can't take these study techniques to improve your marks in the short term on a test or exam, or use them over the years to bring your average up and keep it there. You too can be the "student-athlete" who excels rather than stumbles, who uses these intelligent shortcuts to power your way through your studies to success!

WHERE DID THESE TECHNIQUES COME FROM?

My Life As A Student

During my own long career as a student moving through a bachelor's, master's, and doctoral program, I was able to learn many of these study skills on a "trial and error" basis over the years.

The courses I took over many, many years were difficult and challenging, requiring me to read the material, assimilate it, and respond to it in a meaningful way. In short, to do what all students do.

In addition, there were competitive pressures from professors and classmates—and from me—that "raised the bar" for me to succeed. And, to do so, I had to learn the kinds of "guerrilla study tactics" that would allow me to do the best job possible and get the highest marks I could.

For example, in a particularly tough American Lit class in third-year university, I found myself in a group of twenty or so students at the start of the semester in September. The professor's demands on us were extremely rigorous—she treated us as though we were graduate students in a master's program rather than undergrads.

The pressures were enormous. Each of us had to produce a 15-page essay per semester; we had to present our essay to the class for criticism/evaluation; the essay had to be distributed one week before it was presented in class in order to give everyone enough time to critique it in detail, in a sense to "mark it."

On the day of each presentation, the professor would begin the discussion by analyzing that student's essay herself first. Then each of us would take a turn doing as detailed a job as we could to, in a way, "tear the essay apart." The goal was complex—not only were we trying to comment on the student's efforts in his or her essay, but we were also judged on the basis of our own analysis—in other words, how detailed, how prepared, and how astute our own remarks and insights were.

These sessions were like intense "pressure cookers." And some students didn't handle them. In two months, the course enrollment went from 20 to about 14; by the time we returned to class in January, there were only 11 or 12 left; and by the end of the course in April that number was down to 8 or 9.

Why did so many fall by the wayside? Part of it had to do with some not being able to deal with any aspect of the pressure—of having to produce extremely high-quality work, of having to produce the work in a short time, or of having to criticize the work of their peers in such a vocal and public way. We actually got to the point where, before going into a class, we'd say to that day's presenter (or "victim" as we used to call it), "Don't take this personally," or "I really liked your essay, but I'm going have to say some pretty brutal things about it."

It's easy to see how that kind of situation could take its toll after a while. There were two things that saved me and let me ride out the storm to the end—one was my understanding that, in this special case, I needed to double or triple my focus and study efforts in order to do well; and, two was the simple fact that I would talk things over with a classmate, Garry, just to deal with our emotions around this challenging class.

In fact, we'd often head outside after these classes to Garry's car to talk things over—and even to vent our emotions in a kind of "primal scream." Imagine two grown men sitting in a snow-covered car during a wintry February, our breath fogging the windows, letting out some "rip-roaring" howls just to get the stress, frustration, and sometimes despair out of our systems. This may not sound much like a "technique" or "study strategy" but it did a lot to keep us on an even keel at a time we might otherwise have "burned out" or dropped out.

Three of the issues that have cropped up here—connecting your personality or "self" too closely with your work, the "buddy system," and dealing with your emotions—are important lessons that came out of this experience for me, and they'll be discussed in more detail later in the book.

What I'm happy to say in a positive way about this experience, though, is that I learned more from this course than from almost any other course I ever took. Obviously, I learned much about American Lit and the particular topics that my colleagues and I wrote about. *But I also learned a lot about myself as a learner.* I had to quickly learn *how to learn*—which study habits were useful, which weren't, and how to tell the difference in a "do or die" situation.

My Life As A Professor

The second part of my "learning career" came directly out of my "teaching career." Over the many years I've been a professor, I have taught many students the techniques and strategies that I've written about here.

I've met many students who came to college or university who either had only a faint idea of what to do to improve their marks or none at all. In coming into contact with these students, I've been able to develop and pass on my study skills through my capacities and roles in many educational areas. For instance, over the years, I have been able to help students as a(n):

- professor of writing skills/study skills courses
- seminar leader to other teachers and professors regarding writing and study skills
- professor of courses in Study Skills, Writing, Humanities, Journalism, Media Studies, Literature, and Film Studies
- tutor to students in study skills/writing skills workshops
- evaluator of ESL (English as Second Language) students' language abilities
- enroller/advisor to incoming college and university students
- coordinator/administrator in college and university departments

Through these varied educational functions, I've been fortunate to have opportunities to help students who have been struggling to do their best. And the opportunities themselves have caused me to look long and hard at their situations and ask myself "What can I do to show them how to improve quickly?" and "How can I use my experiences as a student and professor—someone who has been through it all many times over—to turn their struggles into achievements?"

The answers to those questions eventually caused me to write this book—they have spurred me to pass on the strategies, techniques and systems I've used with success to help these many students. I wanted to do this for three reasons:

1. My study skills actually work and work well—I've taken hundreds and thousands of students from low and failing grades to top marks.
2. I want my "insider's" point of view as someone who has been through it all as a student and a professor to help students cut out their trial and error patterns of making the same mistakes over and over.
3. As a teacher in a classroom I can affect the success of only those students who are physically in front of me—writing this book and passing on my "secrets," however, allow me to do what all good teachers want to do, namely to "expand my classroom" and help as many students as possible.

After all, this last reason is why I became a professor in the first place. The old cynical cliché, "Those who can, do; those who can't, teach" has always struck me as an illogical criticism of teaching: "How, I ask, can those who "do" ever have learned to "do" if they weren't taught properly in the first place?"

As a professor, I value learning and teaching—understanding something of value and passing it on—as the greatest skills that anyone can master. They are the bedrock of all societies and the reason that civilizations have evolved into the modern world. And, if we are to continue improving and bettering ourselves, it is only those valuable processes of teaching and learning that will carry on our development.

It's my hope that this book—about how to make students better— will be a small, but worthwhile, contribution to that process.

DO YOU FEEL MOTIVATED TO IMPROVE?

Before we look at actual study strategies, it's important to take a moment to think about the WHY aspect of what it is you're trying to do.

The reason for this is that it's one thing to say "Do these things and you'll get better marks" but quite another to really stop to consider the reasons for wanting to do so in the first place.

You have to feel motivated to want to learn and to want to get top marks before you're willing to learn HOW.

For instance, why do some students "go the distance," do everything they possibly can to succeed in school, while others are content to simply pass or they don't care at all?

The short answer to this is that some are motivated to do their best—they are keenly aware of their goals, the sacrifices they need to make to achieve them, and the need to learn how to achieve them quickly and effectively.

These students have often had to make sacrifices simply to be in high school, college or university in the first place:
- some might have given up a full-time job
- some might have moved out of their parents' home
- some might have given up an independent lifestyle
- some might be single parents
- some might have left their home country

When I speak to such students as these, it's easy to detect their sense of purpose, their focus, and their goals. I hardly ever have to remind them to do this or that, to be on time with their assignments, or to attend class regularly. They simply know what they have to do because—quite clearly—they know why they are doing it.

Other students, the "slackers," may know what they should be doing, but, because they don't have a good reason for doing it, they often don't try or don't care.

So why not start off by testing your motivation to see if you have a sense of purpose and direction? If you do know where you're heading, it'll be that much easier to understand exactly what you'll need to do to get there.

Answer these "motivation questions" to see how much you really are aware of why you're a student—and of what you want to get out of your education.

MOTIVATION SPOT CHECK

Use this rating to answer the following 10 questions:

5 = Strongly Agree
4 = Agree
3 = Don't Know
2 = Disagree
1 = Strongly Disagree

1. I know exactly why I'm in this particular program at high school, college, or university. *1 2 3 4 5*

2. I know how my courses contribute to achieving my goals. *1 2 3 4 5*

3. I know what it takes to do well in my courses. *1 2 3 4 5*

4. I have a positive attitude towards succeeding. *1 2 3 4 5*

5. I associate with classmates who do well in their studies. *1 2 3 4 5*

6. I get along with my teachers/professors. *1 2 3 4 5*

7. I am clear about my career goals. *1 2 3 4 5*

8. I see myself achieving my career goals. *1 2 3 4 5*

9. I prepare for classes, am punctual, attend regularly, take notes, do homework. *1 2 3 4 5*

10. I believe in myself. *1 2 3 4 5*

Scoring—add up your ratings to get a score

41-50 You are highly motivated and focused—you understand your goals clearly and know exactly what it takes to achieve them. You're on the right track!

31-40 You have a fairly clear idea of how what you're doing in school can help you to get where you want to go—just do some fine-tuning to focus some "soft" spots.

21-30 Your motivational skills and goal-setting are at an average

26

level—you need to think in more specific terms about what you're doing and why.

11-20 Your understanding about your career path and goals is low—you need to look carefully at why you are in school and how your program can lead to a specific career.

0-10 You're not at all sure about your goals and why you chose this path at all.

Reading this book will at least help you get a start on clarifying what it takes to succeed in a particular school program.

The answers to these questions will give you the kind of knowledge that you need about yourself even before you're ready to take the "first steps" necessary to get top marks as a student.

They'll tell you if you're already focused on a specific career goal and whether you know how your educational program will lead you to that goal. The greater clarity you have about what you're doing and why you're doing it, the easier it is to apply techniques that will help you to achieve.

SOME TIPS TO HELP YOU BOOST YOUR MOTIVATION

Whether the results of your "Motivation Spot Check" show that you're already highly focused and motivated or whether they tell you that you need a motivation "boost," there are a few simple things that you can do to bring your motivation level up quickly.

Motivation Exercises

Try these ten practical exercises to focus your goals and habits as clearly as possible:

1. *Make a list of career options that interest you.* Write down as many as you can, then   number them from most to least attractive. If you can't think of several possibilities, keep adding to the list over the course of a week or so; if you can't number them right away, then take a few days to think out the order that makes most sense to you. To get yourself "kick started," make

...ointments to talk to people who already work in your field to ...scover the career pros and cons.

Use your top choice from your list to pick an educational program. Once your know the career or job you want, you have a "roadmap" to point you in the right direction. Check out programs at colleges or universities that will lead to the job you've chosen for yourself. Do some research on the Internet to get this information; make appointments with career counselors or student advisors at these institutions. Whatever you decide on, make sure to choose a career that you'll be happy working at— after all, we spend half our lives at work.

3. *Make a list of your strengths.* Knowing something about your pluses is a good way to identify the kinds of character traits you can use to pursue success. For example, identifying such characteristics as "dependable," "organized," "responsible," "punctual," "flexible," "persistent," "dedicated," "creative," and "forgiving" is a great way to find out which qualities you can rely on to get through tough times and to help you stay on course— and writing them down is a good way to regularly remind yourself of your strong points.

4. *Make a list of your weaknesses.* Doing this is a very helpful method of learning about the qualities you need to work on to increase your chances for success. Writing down such points as "lazy," "unfocused," "tardy," "uncooperative," "inconsistent," "forgetful," "disorganized," "thoughtless," and "uncommitted" might not seem like flattering things to admit about yourself. However, being honest about these negative characteristics is a useful start to improving on them.

5. *Write out a list of your goals and objectives.* Try to avoid general statements like "I want to be wealthy" or "money." Instead, zero in on specific things that you would do or have when you have achieved wealth: statements like "I want this kind of house," or "I'd like to travel to Turkey" give you a much clearer picture of your goals—and that kind of image is more realistic to visualize and attain. Another way to do this is to think of specific careers that would let you become wealthy and then narrow your focus on one of them.

6. *Relate your short-term goals to your long-term goals.* If your career goal is to have a career that leads to wealth or job satisfaction, for example, you have identified a long-term goal. Now what you need to do is find out which short-term goals will take you there. For instance, if academic success is the short-

term goal that is key to your long-term goal of career success, then you need to make sure to pay attention to all of the details in your courses that will lead to top marks.

7. *Identify your fears and obstacles.* Jot down a few of the things that could hold you back from achieving your goals. If you acknowledge "I'm a shy person" or "I can't see myself ever amounting to much" or "I don't think I'm smart enough," you're taking the important step of coming face to face with the real or imagined roadblocks that can keep you from where you want to go. And, as with point #4, just putting these negatives on paper is a start to dealing with them.

8. *Believe in yourself and your goals.* Believing in the value of what you want to accomplish and in your ability to accomplish it are no small things. People often have only vague goals at best or they allow others to discourage them from even attempting to fulfill the goals they have. To strengthen your belief level, then, take the two lists you made in exercises #3 and #5, write them out clearly, and place them somewhere (your bathroom mirror, the fridge door) that you'll see them the first thing in the morning and the last thing at night. Revise/rewrite them every few months and keep looking at them regularly.

9. *Visualize your success.* Seeing yourself as successful is the first step in becoming successful. There's an old expression that says "we covet what we see." So if we "see" our success when we close our eyes, in our imagination, or in our mind's eye, then it's only natural to desire that success more all the time. To help yourself do this, you can draw a picture of yourself at graduation or at the job you'll have after you graduate; you can also write a short paragraph of how you would feel at those moments. Make these as specific and detailed as you can.

10. *Take action.* While it's true that thinking about what you want has its own powerful value, it's also inarguable that taking steps to achieving it is essential. Whether we characterize our directed activity as "deeds speak," "he who hesitates is lost," or "action is where the rubber meets the road," the common denominator is clear: our goals will materialize only if we make them happen. As you're choosing a particular educational program, keep a log of the details (appointments, people you meet, information that's helpful)—and do the same as you go through your courses. As you look back at your notebook over the months, you'll see the actual steps you're taking and your confidence and belief will grow when you see the foundation of action you're creating.

MOTIVATION IS THE SPRINGBOARD TO SUCCESS

Your life is the sum result of all the choices you make, both consciously and unconsciously. If you can control the process of choosing, you can take control of all aspects of your life. You can find the freedom that comes from being in charge of yourself.

There is no magic formula for achievement and success in school. There are, however, practical and logical steps that any person can take. But all of the practical and logical advice in the world will only fall on deaf ears if a student isn't focused and motivated.

As you look at these ten steps to help you boost your motivation, you'll notice that all of them require you to make a list or write something down. The reason for this is that, by writing something down, you give it structure.

It's true that the most motivated people are also the most structured people. They see the shape of their goals and the details of the steps they need to take to arrive at them. If you too can start to think and act in terms of structuring your choices and decisions—both small and large—then there's no reason you can't get the top marks, graduate at the top of your class, and find the career that you really want.

NOTES

NOTES

NOTES

NOTES

PART 3

WHAT APPROACH SHOULD YOU TAKE TO STUDYING?

Now that you have a clear idea of exactly why you're in high school, college or university, you also understand the importance of everything you're doing there.

You know, for instance, that every action you take—whether it's taking notes, showing up for class, or doing homework—actually plays a hugely important role in achieving your goals. By themselves, your day-to-day study habits may seem like only small bits of your school routine. But when you add them up, they become the collective "bricks" of the "walls" which are the foundation of your learning.

And, while everyone would probably agree that learning study techniques is crucial to academic success, an overlooked aspect often comes in HOW we go about learning—or in your approach to studying.

As we've just seen, if you tackle studying as well as the rest of your school tasks with the motivated approach we just discussed, then *everything you do will all make sense.* No one will have to explain to you, "Do such and such and it will benefit you." Taking a positive and meaningful approach, you'll understand the purpose of your educational activities as the natural process through which you're passing in your evolution to your career destination.

The alternative approach is not a pleasant one: I've seen too many students through the years who either don't care at all or are just "coasting" through, simply settling for a bare pass mark. What do they look like? They're students who

- don't attend classes or show up only when they feel they have to
- don't buy the textbook
- sit at the back of the classroom so they can "hide"
- don't prepare for class by doing the necessary reading or studying
- casually stroll into class late
- talk during the lecture or class activity
- hand in assignments late or not at all
- don't answer questions at all or are sarcastic in their replies
- make "creative" excuses for their chronic absenteeism
- don't take notes or keep a record of course highlights
- convey a general attitude or boredom, disdain, or indifference

In their minds, these students mostly think that they're being "smart" or "cute" or that they're "faking the teacher out" by putting on a "front" of interest or concern, all the while exhibiting the behaviors on this list. They think that their teacher or professor is actually fooled by their feigned interest and that their charade is somehow going to lead to a positive result for them in that course.

But the opposite is actually the outcome in these situations. Any teacher or professor who has been teaching for any length of time can see through these students. They can easily see the difference between their irresponsible behavior and the behavior of those students who are motivated, focused, and who care deeply about their studies and their results. These are students who

- attend all of their classes and who alert the teacher if they have to be absent
- have the textbook and all the necessary notebooks and materials
- sit as close to the front of the room as possible
- prepare for every class by doing the required reading or studying
- are prompt or in their seats well before the class begins
- pay attention during lectures and speak only when the occasion calls for it

- hand in all assignments on time
- answer questions intelligently and respectfully
- are not chronically absent so they don't require excuses
- take notes and know precisely where the course outcomes are leading them
- convey a general attitude of interest, respect, and involvement

These students are as easy to spot as the opposite ones from the first list. So if students from that list think that they're somehow being "camouflaged"—that we can't tell the "forest from the trees"—they're really only fooling themselves. The contrast between these types of students is so enormous that the "slackers" are just transparent, and it's as easy to detect them as it is to tell the difference between night and day.

YOU DECIDE

Sometimes people will say "But isn't it more complex than just these two extremes? Aren't some students a combination of the two types?"

Well, the truth is that most students are somewhere in between—and in those cases, their marks are usually somewhere in between as well. They're the ones who end up for the most part with C's, while the slackers get the D's and F's, and the top students get the A's and B's.

While these average students are certainly more conscientious than the slackers, they also often lack something possessed by the students in the top category. They're in a kind of "gray zone" in the middle, striving to improve their assignments and marks, but falling short of that upper zone perhaps because of a lack of motivation or a weakness in their writing skills or study skills.

Unfortunately, this group represents the majority of students in any high school, college or university. They're the students who don't do poorly enough to fail, but who also don't do well enough to achieve the top marks. They struggle to get through their courses and, more often than not, have to settle for marks that could have been—and should have been—better. Well, there is some good news here. If you're one of these students in this middle category and if you've been looking for something to get you into that top group, then just do these two things:

1) take the motivation test in Part 2 of this book to increase your focus on your goals
2) follow closely the strategies, tips, techniques, and hints in the rest of this book to pull yourself into the top zone of student performers

It's up to you to decide which type of student represents you—top, bottom or middle—and it's up to you to decide what steps you're going to take to improve.

The choice is yours—it's really only you who knows where you've been, where you are, and where you're heading. And it's really only you who can decide whether you're prepared to do what it takes to get you there.

THE FIRST STEP – LONG-TERM STUDY STRATEGIES

Success isn't an elevator—it's a stairway you take one step at a time.

If you really are committed to achieving your goals, if you're clear about how your studies are the path to career success—it's now time for you to take the first step in that direction. Also, if you agree that working within a pattern or structure that gives shape to your actions is a good idea, then it's time to talk about the structure that long-term study strategies provide.

Your long-term study strategy can apply to the length of your program (usually two, three, or four years) or to the length of your semester (usually 4 or 8 months)—which is usually the length of any given course.

What this means is that over the long-term of either your program or your course(s), you're looking at what you need to do to put into place a "game plan" for how you are going to study to get top marks.

You've already decided that you're sufficiently motivated and focused, that you have all your reasons in place for why you're going to succeed in school—now you just need to think about HOW you're going to succeed.

"PLAN THE WORK— THEN WORK THE PLAN"

This often-quoted statement carries a large element of truth if you're interested in getting results from your study goals. "Planning the work" refers, of course, to *thought* while "working the plan" means taking *action*. Thought and action; thoughtful action; active thought. These are all ways of saying the same important thing: that if you first lay out what it is you're going to do—and then follow up by actually doing it—you have a strong chance of achieving success.

It's important to see here, that one without the other isn't good enough. On the one hand, a student can have a great student plan, but do absolutely nothing about it; while, on the other hand, another student can appear "active" by running off in all directions, but having all that energy not actually achieve any results.

So, let's step back and take a look at the overall "big picture" of how a long-term study strategy can work for you.

THINK OF A SOARING EAGLE LOOKING DOWN

A long-term study plan begins with a vantage point or a perspective on what it is you want to accomplish.

If you think of an eagle that's flying overhead and looking down, what do you think the eagle sees? Well, the answer probably has to do with a "big view" or "large perspective" of the landscape. It doesn't see the small blades of grass or individual tress, but it does see the large meadows and vast forests.

At the start of your program, you are like that eagle, looking not at the content of any particular course or what will be on a specific test, but rather looking at the expanse of your entire program, at what the whole 4 or 6 semester stack of courses looks like. From this perspective, then, you get the "big picture" of what you'll be tackling over the next two or three years.

There are several advantages to looking at things like this:
- it allows you to take stock of exactly what awaits you in each semester
- it lets you determine the degree of difficulty among semesters
- it gives you a chance to prepare for a semester
- it prompts you to judge how to spend your time in a semester

TAKE STOCK OF EACH SEMESTER

Being able to look at the list of courses that you'll be taking in any semester gives you the opportunity to know what it is you're facing. This might sound a bit obvious, but when you think about it, many times students arrive at college or university with only a vague idea of what they're enrolled in and only later come to discover that there is a math, or science, or humanities component they didn't know about.

What kind of surprise could this turn out to become if you happen to be weak in one of those areas; and how could that "weakness" affect the outcome of your marks or your Grade Point Average?

Knowing exactly what it is you're up against can give you a huge advantage when you come to tackle your workload.

Let's take a look at an example of this list of required courses for a first semester Financial Planning Program:

Accounting Principles I
Business Writing I
Fundamentals to Financial Planning
Introduction to Business
Computer Skills and Applications
Database Concepts and Design

What you see in this list is a "snapshot" of *exactly* which courses you're going to have to take right away. And this snapshot can help you enormously by leading you to ask important "assessment questions" about your situation:

"What do I know about financial planning to help me in that course?"

"Have I read some articles or books on it, spoken to people in the field, or worked in that area before?"

"How about that accounting course—what's my experience here? How do I feel about my math abilities?"

"And what about my business writing course? Am I comfortable with my communications skills and writing ability to do well here?"

These kinds of evaluation questions can open the door for your critical, objective and necessary understanding of what you're going to need to do in order to achieve success.

JUDGE THE DEGREE OF DIFFICULTY AMONG SEMESTERS

At the same time you also need to look ahead at what you'll be facing in upcoming semesters.

Take a look at this sample of Financial Planning courses for semester 2:

Accounting Principles II
Business Writing II
Advanced Financial Planning
Money Management and Application Software
Spreadsheet Concepts and Design
Retirement and Estate Planning

What you immediately see about the courses in this list is that some of them are extensions of courses in semester one, while others are completely different.

For starters, this means that you're going to have to continue to ask the same kinds of assessment questions about these semester two courses in order to get a handle on them.

In addition, your assessment will also likely lead you to conclude is that semester two courses look even more difficult than those in semester one. This means that your study strategies for semester two have to be even more focused than they were before.

For example, you could look at taking one or two semester two courses that were available, say, over the summer *before* semester two begins—this way, you lighten your study load when you get into semester two. This type of "spreading out" of your courses increases the amount of time you can physically give to all of your courses, decreases the stress factor, and increases your probabilities for getting higher marks.

The bonuses of this kind of strategy are easily apparent—so be sure to do this same kind of evaluating with semesters three and four, and, if necessary, with any others in your particular program.

HOW TO PREPARE FOR A SEMESTER

This point is an extension of the previous one on "taking stock of each semester." Starting with the types of questions you were asking there, move on to even more specific ones that will shape your actions for each course.

For instance, if you answered "I really don't know anything about the details of what I can expect in a financial planning course," you have some work cut out for yourself if you expect to do well in that course.

Or, if you said to yourself that "Yikes! I haven't written an essay or business letter in the past 5 years, so I don't know how I'll do," you also have to take charge and prepare yourself to get a head start.

I have seen a big difference in the results of students who have done these types of assessments (and then taken some action even before the courses start) and those who walk in the first day and say "Gee, I wonder what this course will be all about?" It's not to say that this kind of student could never do well—it's just that the odds of getting top marks increases with the amount of preparation and forethought.

Here are some things you can do to put yourself in the best position:
- find out which textbooks you'll need for each course and get them as early as you can—read as much as possible *before* the course begins
- get course outlines for each course as early as possible—these are often printed well in advance of the start of the course (check with each department)
- make an appointment with as many professors as possible before each course starts—find out as much as you can about the course
- locate the important academic facilities on the campus: computer rooms, study areas, resource rooms, and professors' offices
- identify key locations of registrar's office, financial aid office, career counseling, peer tutoring, bookstore, copier services, cafeteria
- purchase all your notebooks, binders, calculators, pens and pencils early to avoid having to stand in long lineups once the semester starts (this is tougher when you're waiting for financial aid, but do what you can to avoid losing time)
- get your locker, student ID, and computer passwords settled early
- go to all your orientation sessions to speak to professors to

find out about your schedule and courses
- craft a sensible timetable for yourself when you're registering online (if you're not a "morning person," don't slot in all early classes)

While some of these are admittedly "housekeeping" items, it's smart to clear them out of the way to free up all of your time for studying. I don't know too many students who ever achieved high grades for knowing the combination to their locker or for spending all their time in the campus pub!

HOW TO SPEND YOUR TIME IN A SEMESTER

Knowing that you could be weak in math, for example, is an important first step in being able to do something about your weakness.

If you're faced with an accounting or a math course and you feel threatened by it or sense that it will pull your marks down rather than up, you know that you'll have to find some help for yourself when the semester starts.

It's best to do this even before classes begin. And you can do this by finding the math tutoring center (where professors tutor students), the peer tutoring office (where students tutor other students), or any other remediation resources that your college or university has (just be sure to ask and look for them).

What you're doing here is judging your strengths and weaknesses in various courses and making important and necessary distinctions about where it is you need to spend more or less time. Not all courses are the same. If you're stronger in writing skills and weaker in math, then it's clear that spending less time in one can afford you the extra time you'll need to spend in order to do well in the other.

The need to achieve a balance is often overlooked by students who look at all of their courses and think that they have to spend an equal amount of time in each of them—and then end up with lopsided results.

THE BENEFITS OF OUR LONG-TERM APPROACH

Many times, students have said to me that there's a difference to them between "need to do" and "nice to do" strategies. By this, they differentiate between those absolutely essential techniques and those—like the ones in our discussion of long-term planning—that they might find useful, but only marginally so. They think that they simply need to show up at the start of the term, jump right in, and "ace" their courses without any kind of pre-thinking or long-term strategies.

To this I can truly say that, in today's highly competitive educational and career worlds, the successful people are the structured ones. And these are people who don't underestimate the edge that any element of forethought and structure might give them over someone else.

It's much like hiring a carpenter to build you a house, but not providing a blueprint for how you want it built. You would probably be as displeased with that result as you would be if you're a student without a plan, just floundering around from course to course, hoping that something good will come out of it.

Planning ahead and taking responsibility for your plan are the hallmarks of successful people and of students who get the top marks. They're the perspective of that eagle who looks down and always has a eye on the entire landscape and a sense of direction.

You can judge your own view by this saying: "Some people make things happen. Some people wait for things to happen. And then there are those who say—*what happened?*"

NOTES

NOTES

NOTES

NOTES

PART 4

MEDIUM-TERM STUDY STRATEGIES

Now that you have a good sense about how to do the best with your program and your courses over the long term, it's time to consider what you need to do in what we can call the medium term—over the length of a course.

The key here is to be able to say, "I've been able to get a head start on my courses by preparing. I got the textbook beforehand and read the first few chapters, I have the course outline and know what the highlights are, and I'm now ready to walk in for the first class."

Certainly, if you've done all this, you're as prepared to do well as you possibly can be. It's like the difference between going to a party and having to figure things out as you go along, or experiencing the "comfort zone" of going to one where you know everyone and consequently feel relaxed and sure of yourself.

You also have a certain degree of comfort from the assurance that you know what you need to do well in all of your courses over this semester as well as over the length of your entire program. That's great.

Imagine for a moment the opposite picture. You don't really know why you're in this program (no long term goals), you haven't got a clear idea of why you're taking these particular courses or how they're meant to help you (no motivation), and you haven't done any planning or preparing (no long-term study strategy). How comfortable can you feel in this situation?

The reality is, though, that too many students are arriving in just that condition—missing all or most of these pluses. And they're the majority who end up like the students described in Part 3—"playing a game" with their education and finally failing, dropping out, or just barely scraping by.

But that doesn't have to be you. If you just follow these straightforward steps and start to form "study habits" over the length of any course, you can be one of those students who sees success in the classroom—success in your medium-term study strategy.

THE VALUE OF LECTURES

Because you now know WHY you're taking these steps, at this point you need to know HOW to take them.

Class lectures are a prime way for teachers and professors to convey important information to you. Unfortunately, many students have only a dim idea of why they sit in lectures or, worse yet, no idea at all. They sometimes think that lectures are just a waste of time ("This info isn't really that important") or that they're just a "rehash" of what they already know ("I already read that stuff in the text"). What they often miss is the fact that lectures serve extremely useful functions:

- they serve to highlight the most important ideas and concepts in a course
- they create a framework for the pre-class reading you've done
- they give students an opportunity to provide some feedback to those ideas
- they allow for "dialogues" or interactions around those concepts and ideas

- they're a signal to students as to what they can expect to see on a test or exam

Lectures, then, have an incredibly powerful function as a focusing device for the course. Once students know this, they can come to see lectures as a useful and helpful tool in their medium-term strategy. And effective note taking is the key to capturing the value of your lectures.

TAKING GOOD NOTES

1) *Write down important words and phrases that your professor emphasizes.* Learn to watch for cues as to what is considered important. Not everything that's said in a lecture is equally important, so learn to distinguish the key ideas from introductory, transitional or supporting remarks. When something is written on the board or overhead, for example, you should see that as a big signal. Also, watch out for when points are introduced by signaling phrases: "the main factor is...," "five significant causes are...," and "the main conclusion we can draw...." Another clue can also be the way in which the main points are conveyed by the professor—speaking more clearly, loudly or slowing are often effective means to verbally "underline" something essential.

2) *Use your own shorthand system.* Too often, students think they need to write down everything that's said in a lecture rather than focus on only the key points. Besides, you'd never be able to copy everything word for word that your professor says in a lecture—your hand would cramp up in no time at all! So your only sensible alternative is to write down just the key words and phrases while using "shortcuts" for the connecting/relating functions. A few examples of these could be = (equals), ex (for example), > (greater than), < (less than), ! (important), ? (question), n.g. (no good), etc. (and so forth). This technique can save you a lot of time and let you continue to focus on the most important parts of the lecture.

3) *Use key words to cluster the main points.* Identify the key words of the lecture as you're hearing it, and then write them down in your notebook with plenty of space around each of them. When the details about a particular key word are discussed, write them down in a kind of circle format around that word much like the shape of the planets orbiting around

the sun. When you do this for the various key points of the lecture, you'll end up with groupings or clusters of information—with the details surrounding the key points. This makes it easy for you to identify and connect relationships in terms of primary and secondary levels of importance.

4) *Or use an outline format for your notes.* An alternative to the "cluster" system for note taking is an outline format. Your main heading would be a particular concept, then your subheadings under it would consist of supporting ideas, definitions, and sub-points. You would line up your main point with the left-hand margin, then indent all of the supporting data to readily identify the order of importance among these ideas. You can try both the cluster and outline techniques to see which one works better for you.

5) *Bring your textbook to class with you.* Your professor will often refer to information contained in the textbook so it's definitely a bonus if you have yours there to reinforce that concept and where it's located. As well, it's effective to use as a handy reference source for a quick "brush up" of a concept that's being discussed—you can easily look up a key term that you might have forgotten for a moment. Just be careful not to "get lost" by drifting away and reading your textbook when you should be focusing on the lecture.

6) *Write neatly enough so that you can read it later.* It's extremely frustrating after your lecture when you discover that you can't read half of what you've spent so much energy writing down! To avoid this kind of wasted effort, be sure to "write it so you can read it." The clue here is in the fact that you will almost never write down any kind of sentences at all from the lecture (although students always seem to try to do this). Even during a short one-hour lecture, trying to write down any sentences from the professor—whether long or short—is a recipe for disaster (writer's cramp and frustration are the only consequences of this). Stick to brief words and phrases instead, and make them legible by printing or writing clearly.

7) *Leave wide margins around what you write.* If you try to cram everything tightly onto your pages, you'll end up with notes that are hard to read and you'll have nowhere to add something that comes up later in the lecture. Leave at least a wide margin on the left side of the page to add a late comment to a particular cluster or key concept—or to add a point or

connection that occurred to you.

8) *Don't forget to label, number and date all your notes.* Keeping track of what you've written and when you wrote it is an organizational tool you can use to your advantage. This also allows to you effectively segment your notes into "time" and "content" groupings which will make it easier for you to identify which segments you'll need to focus on when it comes time to prepare for either a tightly-focused test or a more broadly focused mid-term or final exam.

9) *Use either dedicated notebooks or three-ring binders for each course.* Never, ever, use one or two notebooks for all of your class notes for all of your courses. This kind of jumbled approach to cataloging your valuable information will only end up creating confusion by overlapping or omitting course content from several courses when what you really want to do is to create a separate and discrete "working unit" for each course. You can do this using either a separate notebook or a three-ring binder for each course, but a loose-leaf binder gives you greater flexibility by allowing you to add/remove/rearrange notes, handouts and other inserts as the course develops (this could also be a useful feature when it comes time to studying from a particular segment of notes).

10) *Review your notes as soon as possible.* Sometimes students think "I've just taken down these notes and they're here on these pages, so why do I have to look at them until I need to study?" There are actually several benefits to taking a bit of time to examine your notes as soon as possible after or even during a class: for one, it allows you to check for errors, omissions, and possible connections—it lets you "fill in the blanks" in what you've written; for another, it lets you reinforce those key points and concepts—good retention begins with solid review techniques. Taking a few minutes at the end of the day is an opportunity for you to adjust, edit or even re-write parts of the lecture so that you further sharpen your focus on the important details of a course.

11) *Take notes from your notes.* This important strategy is not meant to sound confusing. What it refers to is this: take a few minutes each day to highlight key points from your lecture notes onto an index card. Gather these cards for each course and review them at the end of each week (this needn't require much time to do). What you'll gradually develop is a tightly focused "profile" of highlights that will help you create a

structure for what is important in any given course. Add one more step: at the end of each month, cluster your index cards into a pile and then go through them looking for key concepts and terms that come up with regularity. This "frequency factor" creates a pattern that tells you that these are the areas you should be spending most of your time on.

12) *Be sure to obtain lecture notes from a classmate if you miss a class.* If the rare occasion occurs in which you absolutely have to miss a class, make sure to get a copy of someone else's notes. While these won't be as good as having your own notes, at least you'll have a sense of the overall picture of that class. Also, ask some questions of that student about the key points that were stressed by the professor—it's better to have some idea of what was highlighted than none at all.

13) *Pros and cons of using a laptop computer to take notes.* Because students are increasingly taking laptop or notebook computers to class, you may want to use one yourself to take your lecture notes. There are several advantages to this: your notes will be more legible; you can easily add/insert more material later; and revision and editing will be that much easier. There are also some disadvantages, though: there is a loss of flexibility by your not being able to add margin notes; it's harder to add formulas, graphs, or even to highlight as quickly as you may need to. Your decision to use a laptop for note-taking purposes is really dependent upon your comfort level with it and your ability to make these kinds of adjustments.

14) *Share notes if you're working in a study group.* Sometimes it's an effective study strategy for you to use a "buddy system" with one or more other students in the same class. After a class or during a break, you can all spend a few minutes exchanging your views on what you thought was important in the lecture. It's always eye-opening to hear what someone else caught and you missed; it's also revealing to learn someone else's slant on an idea you had already made your mind up about. In addition, you could further benefit from such a group by meeting to form practice test questions for each other, set up mini-debate forums, or focus on each student's index cards to see if you're picking up on the same key concepts.

Why are we spending all this time on the techniques for effective note taking?

You want to come to see your notes as the bridge between the beginning and the end of your course. They capture the ideas, theories, concepts, and highlights of a course and, if you do the required work to "join the dots" among these, your notes will allow you to create a "roadmap" of the course. You can then use that map to point yourself in all kinds of helpful directions: particularly towards determining the nature and types of questions you're likely to see on any tests and exams for that course.

Also, learn to guard your notes carefully because, if you lose them, what you've really done is lose your course. True, your textbook is important, but only in the sense that it gives you all the "raw data" for that course—your notes take that data and give you a special opportunity to put a structure to it.

I have seen some students use this medium-term strategy to take them through a course with great success. But I've also seen many others who didn't have a plan, who didn't take notes at all, who tried to "fake" or "bluff" their way through, and ended up just guessing when a test or exam arrived—"hoping and groping" for a good result. These students were almost always disappointed, but the ones with the roadmap of their notes most often got the good marks they planned for.

WHERE DO YOU DO YOUR BEST STUDYING?

Knowing which environment you perform best in is as helpful as knowing how to use your notes effectively.

Some students say "I absolutely need a quiet place to study" while others say "I can study with the radio and the TV going." And, in a way, both are right. Each type of student has already figured out if noises or other kinds of commotion are distracting or not.

In the same way, every individual student should make similar judgments about all of the following environment features to decide which "study space" is the correct one. There are no "right" or "wrong" answers to these points—but what's crucial here is knowing your work habits, attention span and pet peeves well enough to be able to make the most productive choices for yourself:

- *Do you prefer a "private" or a "public" space?* Private study spaces are those at home, usually your own room or a den.

Public spaces can range from your best friend's room to the library to include even public transit or a city park.

- *Is your space neat, organized and well equipped?* Spending time looking for class notes in "one of the piles at the foot of my bed" can put a big dent in the 40 minutes you allotted for studying those notes. Similarly, wasting time looking for or simply not having your study tools—notes, textbook, pens, paper, pencils, markers, dictionary, thesaurus, calculator and computer—can easily wipe out all kinds of good intentions of getting important work done. The saying "a place for everything and everything in its place" didn't become a valuable truth for no reason.

- *Do your comfort requirements interfere with your productivity needs?* Studying for tests and exams is a rigorous activity that requires all of your focus and concentration. Relaxing on your bed to go over your textbook or notes may seem like a good idea ("at least I'll be comfortable while I'm reading"), but too often the tendency to doze or at least to diminish your level of concentration will take over. The same applies to comfy sofas and easy chairs. Look at it this way: if you wouldn't think of driving a car while stretched on a mattress, why would you do that when studying? Find a firm but comfortable chair, use a sufficiently large desk, make sure you have clear overhead lighting, and see that your area is well ventilated.

- *Is your study space a distraction zone?* When concentration is vital, there are two possible "intruders" that can upset it—you yourself and anyone else. If you choose to study in a room that's also your "entertainment center," equipped with TV, sound system and the Internet, it's easy to see how the shift from studying to "I'll just take some downtime with this new CD" can occur. And, when it isn't you who is responsible for the distraction, it could easily be someone else. So, disconnect the phone line, turn your cell phone off, inform others of your study times, or hang a "please do not disturb sign" on your door handle. Do whatever it takes to stay in control of this time and place.

- *Have you considered using the library occasionally?* If you prefer studying in the library anyway, this is easy enough to answer. High school, college, university and public libraries are perfect study places. They're full of books, magazines, and journals—all the resource material you'll require—and these days they come complete with Internet access if you don't have it at home. You can usually find a well-lit study desk with functional seating and not be disturbed by the generally low level of noise. Even students who usually prefer to study at home have said that working the library into their study schedule—say, for one day a week—has created some variety in their study pattern and has given them a useful study place.

- *Do you control your study space or does it control you?* Regardless of which physical space you choose to study in, it's also important that you have a kind of "mental" control over it. What this means is that, for the length of time that you're in that space to study, you should be determined to fulfill your purpose by actually studying. Look at his example: if you study in your bedroom—which is actually a multi-purpose environment you use for sleeping, watching TV, listening to the radio, talking on the phone, visiting with friends—when it comes time to study, you're not actually in a dedicated study environment. Therefore, to help yourself focus on your purpose at that time, why not use a visual trick to help you SEE your function in that room at that time? Print a sign that reads "STUDY ROOM" in bold letters and put it up when you start to study and then take it down each time you finish studying. This also works in the library when it might be easy to become distracted talking to other students. The sign is your visual cue as to your purpose and it lets you control your study environment.

When your study environment is of your choosing and it suits your particular learning habits, then you've done all you can to ensure that the physical part of the study process is more "helpful" than "harmful" to the result.

HOW DO YOU MANAGE STUDY TIME?

There's an old Rolling Stones' song called *Time Is On My Side*—and the main point of the lyrics is that, when used wisely, time always is our ally.

When I've given out an assignment that's due in a week I've heard some students say, "Hey, that's not enough time," while others said, "No sweat." Why the difference in response? Well, it's clear that if the length of time was the same for both types of students, the only difference came from how they saw their use of that time span.

Another critical aspect of time management is this: no matter how much time some students have to complete something, it never seems as if it's enough. Conversely, others can take as little time as an evening or a few days and end up doing an incredibly good job.

There's no magical formula to dealing with how to make the best use of our time except to say that it has to do with *organization* and *developing habits*. These two "mindsets" have almost everything to do with the constructive use of study time. If you are able to 1) organize your time efficiently and 2) repeat useful study habits, you'll be able to get the maximum productivity from your effort.

Here are some concrete "time tips" that students have successfully used:

- *Plan your study time.* Whether you delegate as little as 30 minutes for a particular study session or up to 2-3 hours or more, have a clear idea of exactly what you want to achieve. As well, set out the order in which you're going to work and see that your study goals are achievable in that time frame.

- *Use your study sessions to go over your valuable lecture notes.* Earlier, we looked at the importance of taking good notes as the basis of your medium-term study plan in order to put yourself in a good position. A week before a test or exam, you can now focus on reviewing the most relevant concepts, ideas, key points and supporting details because you've created a meaningful structure of information for yourself throughout the course. This is much better than randomly trying to guess what's important.

- *Establish a priority sequence for each study session.* Spend a few minutes at the start of each session to categorize what it is you need to learn from MOST to LEAST important. Write down a short list of these points in that order, and then look at it as you study to actually "see" yourself moving through the list. Another advantage here is the fact that you're breaking your task down into smaller, more manageable parts, rather than leaving it as one vague and large "chunk."

- *Study any topic that you consider to be "difficult" or "boring" first.* The logic of tackling these kinds of subjects first lets you lighten your study load as you go. If you save the "heavy" areas for last, the danger is that you'll never get to them. Also, watch for subjects that you avoid studying—that's usually a signal of a problem area.

- *When possible, make your study time your "best" time of the day, the time that you feel fresh and alert.* For some students, that time is in the morning, for others, it's the evening. Obviously, you need to account for duties, errands, chores or part-time jobs, but making adjustments to allow yourself to be in top form for your study time will be a huge benefit.

- *Recognize and use "down time" productively.* "Down time" is any time that you spend waiting. This can be travel time spent on a bus or subway, time waiting in a doctor's office, or even a few moments during lunch or class breaks. Many students spend time reading transit ads or listening to music when they could be using those valuable minutes to scan their notes or to review a difficult chapter in the text.

- *Try to alternate the material you're studying.* For example, if you have two tests coming up at about the same time, divide your study time to cover them both and to avoid "tuning out" or losing focus. You can do this in a 2-hour study session, say, by spending the first half hour on your Math notes, the second half hour on Business Writing, the third half hour on Math, and then the last block on the Business Writing material again.

- *There's another good reason to alternate your study material:* studies show that maximum attention span is only about 20 minutes (about the length of a half-hour TV show minus the commercials). Use this as a guideline whether you're switching content from different courses (as in the previous point) or you're alternating from studying notes, to textbook, to Internet material for the same course. Whichever timeframe you use, don't go for over an hour studying the same way or the same material.

- *Know how to make the best use of break times.* Breaks are not only your small "rewards" for hard work, but they're also necessary interruptions to get you to change your posture, activity and rhythm. If you've been sitting at your desk and reading, for instance, then during your break you should be standing, walking, or moving around. The old saying, "A change is good as a rest" definitely fits here—you should feel recharged and refocused if you've made your break time different from your study time. How long should your break be? What works well for most students is a 10-minute break for every hour of studying—any more frequently than that and it might be too hard for you to return from your break.

- *Finally, make a pattern or a habit of your study times.* Once you know what works best for you in terms of structuring your study times, use that pattern over again and again. Don't be reluctant to make adjustments when necessary or to refine how you use this valuable time.

The chief benefit of learning how to use your time to study is a simple but important one: you are now able to exercise an element of control over how you deal with studying for a test or an exam. The next time you hear your teacher or professor say "And I know you'll be prepared for next week's test on these chapters," you should have the reassurance that you know how to spend your time to prepare. That's much better than the uncertainty that comes from wondering what you're going to do and trying to guess at when you're going to do it.

SHOULD YOU USE A STUDY GROUP?

The power of many is greater than the power of one.

There are many advantages that come from studying in a group. Not the least of these is the fact that it's often easier to achieve something in a group than it is on your own.

Some of this is, of course, a result of perception. There has long existed a kind of idealized student-scholar image of the "lone wolf" student, grappling on an individual basis with the challenging demands of higher learning. Many students relate to this image and thus might be reluctant to seek out others with whom to spend time studying.

But if the circumstances are right for you to form or to join a study group, you'll benefit from the synergy that comes from working with other responsible students. You'll be able to gain a level of energy that comes from the dynamics of the group's interaction as well as raise your level of commitment to your work that comes from being accountable to others.

You can usually spot a few students in any class that you would want to work with. They're often the ones who ask intelligent questions, whose comments show that they've read the material and are prepared, and whose overall approach to the course shows that they're in class to genuinely learn. It's easy enough to speak to them before or after class and then to exchange phone numbers or e-mail addresses and set up a first meeting.

You can work out a schedule for your study group on a weekly basis, and then benefit from the following activities:

- *Compare highlights of the notes that each of you has taken individually in class.* Doing this lets you create a consensus on the important issues in a particular chapter or section. If several students are coming up with the same points, that's a strong indication that questions about these points are likely material to appear on a test.

- *Pool your resources to create "strength in numbers."* Group members can identify whatever books, articles, journals and Internet sources they've found helpful. Chances are good that a variety of these will emerge and help to build a "study bank" of resources that's available to all group members.

- *Formulate possible test questions.* Each student can take a turn and come up with one question on each key issue that's discussed that day. Then the rest of the group can work together to brainstorm the best possible answers. The result of several students giving their view of the same answer expands the range of possibilities that any one student could have come up with alone.

- *Practice teaching the material to the group.* Take turns preparing "mini lectures" for upcoming sessions to teach the highlights of an important concept to the group. Verbalizing the material allows you to reinforce it by actually "talking it out" rather than just thinking about it. Students' confidence usually grows in these situations because they take control of their ideas by presenting them. It's also a good idea to be prepared to take feedback and to answer questions from your audience.

- *Use the "game show" approach to create a question-and-answer format to study for multiple-choice tests.* Take turns playing the "host" who makes up short, factual questions about dates, places, people, inventions, and so on. You can choose either a random or ordered selection of "contestants" who try to get the right answer. You can even have "prizes" of snacks, fruit or nuts, or pretend "bonus test marks" to give out for the correct answer.

- *Do "talk show" interviews on chapters or readings.* Take turns playing "host" and "guest" with the guest giving a synopsis of a specific chapter, say, and the host then asking questions or further details about it.

- *Divide the group into teams and stage debates.* Be sure to alternate members each time so that teams are flexible rather than set. These debates can be based on differing viewpoints of the material and again give the benefit of expanding the range of perspectives coming from the group.

- *Celebrate your victories.* In "debriefing" meetings following a test or exam, be sure to acknowledge the successes of other group members and of the group as a whole. Success is "contagious" in a positive way and many students have pleasantly discovered that being part of a student study enterprise resulted in a significant improvement in their marks.

Another real benefit of group work beyond raising your marks is, of course, the experience itself. Most careers these days involve a strong element of teamwork. The cooperative learning skills that you gain now from working in a study group also play an important part in your becoming a good "team player" on the job. This is an appealing consequence of group work that some students tend not to see, but forward-thinking students are aware of such "ripple" benefits that can help them later as well as now.

NOTES

NOTES

NOTES

NOTES

PART 5

SHORT-TERM STUDY STRATEGIES

Short-term study strategies basically consist of the things you need to do to prepare yourself when a test or exam is coming up. The timeframe is tight in these situations with perhaps only a week or less to go and you're thinking of which specific strategies would effectively reduce your anxiety and increase your level of preparedness.

As we've seen before with long-term and medium-term study strategies, having a plan, approach, strategy, or technique with which to tackle your task is far better and more effective than not. In the same way, students who lack a structured approach to short-term studying are not in a position to do well. I've seen them over the years at test time either wondering what to do and hoping for the best, or simply assuming that "it will all come back to me" at the appropriate moment.

That's not to say that such students might not pass the test or exam—in fact, they may remember enough material or their high stress levels may cause them to focus enough to get through with a passing mark. But is this what they or anyone else could call a productive learning experience or a successful result?

Well, it can hardly be termed a "successful learning experience" if you're not in control of the situation (as much as you reasonably can be). What preparation really does is allow you the opportunity to reduce uncertainty and risk. When you step into an exam experiencing a high level of control because you know the material, you've pre-thought the possible questions through your thorough note taking, and you used a short-term study strategy, you've realistically done your best to bring down the level of unpredictability as close to zero as possible.

For the students who go in "winging it," unpredictability is all they have. That's why, whatever questions they encounter, whatever information they're asked for, and whatever pressures they feel because they didn't prepare, everything works to turn that situation into a recipe for disaster. So it's little wonder that a "successful result" (which we could hardly call a bare pass) is something that could come from this—it's just not reasonable to expect a "predictably" good result from "unpredictable" and poor preparation.

So, in order to get the best possible results from what you CAN control, start by looking at what you want to achieve and decide on the best way to get you there.

ASSESS YOUR NEEDS

Assessing your needs to develop a short-term study strategy can function on several levels. You'll need to examine such things as:
- What kind of learner are you?
- Do you have a study system?
- How do you deal with test stress?
- Do you tend to procrastinate?
- Do you have a preparation checklist?

What you're actually trying to do in these situations is maximize your time and effort. If you break down your task into these categories and then excel in each of them, the overall effect should be highly positive.

WHAT KIND OF LEARNER ARE YOU?

It's very much a proven fact that all students don't learn the same way. I have students in my classes who are very good listeners and they're able to identify the emphasis in my voice at different times—when I repeat a point, speak more loudly about an idea, or lower my voice to suggest a change in direction. They "pick up" these distinctions on an auditory level and then either write down that point or focus more intently on the discussion. I know this simply by looking at how they react in front of me.

Other students are more visual types of learners. They take in information best when it's presented to them visually through pictures and images. When I present material through overheads, charts, films or class demonstrations, these students would respond more than others by asking questions and engaging in discussion—they were reacting much more than others to the visual nature of the content.

A third learning style is called kinesthetic, and this type of student learns best through tactile or "hands on" interaction. Any classroom activity that stresses "doing"—experiments, demonstrations, group activities, labs—falls into this category. Such students take in information best when they are engaged as part of the learning process in an active, participatory way.

Learning Types Spot Check

Answer the following questions to find out which type of learner you are. Use the following rating system to get your score:

Mostly (5)   Sometimes (3)   Rarely (1)

Auditory (Listening) Learner

1. I find it easy to take notes during a lecture.   *5 3 1*

2. Writing is easy for me and my handwriting is
   neat and clear.   *5 3 1*

3. I would rather learn through listening than by reading. *5 3 1*

4. I usually remember something when I hear it.   *5 3 1*

5. I really enjoy listening to the radio and hearing
   tapes and CDs.   *5 3 1*

Visual Learner

1. Watching the professor closely seems to help me learn.   *5 3 1*

2. I get the point easier when it's written down or on an overhead.   *5 3 1*

3. I would rather learn through reading than by listening.   *5 3 1*

4. I usually remember something when I see it.   *5 3 1*

5. I really enjoy watching TV or movies.   *5 3 1*

Kinesthetic ("Hands On") Learner

1. I prefer to move around rather than sit still during a lecture.   *5 3 1*

2. I really enjoy group discussions and activities.   *5 3 1*

3. I prefer to learn by doing rather than by reading or listening.   *5 3 1*

4. I usually remember something when try it for myself.   *5 3 1*

5. I enjoy sports and physical activity in general   *5 3 1*

Add up your scores for each of these categories of learning types. A score of 20+ indicates strength in that learning type; a score of 10-20 is moderate; and a score from 0-10 is low.

You may notice several things from your scores:
- You likely show strength in one of the three areas. The benefit here is that you now know which area to build on and which you can rely on during lectures, tests and exams.
- You might also score high in two or even all three learning types. What this result tells you is that you are a versatile learner who can take in information well on several levels—a definite bonus when it comes to studying.
- Knowing what your low-scoring areas are is also helpful. You now know to avoid study techniques that might hinder you, while at the same time learn how to improve those weaker skills.

Students are rarely ever only one type of learner—everyone seems to possess various degrees of strengths and weaknesses. There is a real benefit here, though, beyond just knowing what your personal strengths and weaknesses as a learner are—it comes in knowing how to use your strengths to study better and how to avoid situations in which your weaknesses could harm your results.

Students learn 10% of what they read, 20% of what they hear, 30% of what they see, 50% of what they see and hear, 70% of what is discussed with others, 80% of what they experience personally, and 95% of what they teach to someone else.

DO YOU HAVE A STUDY SYSTEM?

Taking an organized approach to how you study is an important way to ensure that you use your study time as efficiently as you can. The difference between students who are prepared to write a test or exam and those who aren't has a lot to do with establishing for themselves, and repeating, certain steps in the study process:

- *Use index cards, highlighters, and colored notebooks to create "color structures" for yourself.* Try to use a color code binder system to identify courses— "red" is for your History course, "green" is for Math, "blue" is for English, and so on. You can do the same by using colored floppy disks or CD-ROMs for different courses—but, if you can't, always label everything boldly and clearly.

- *Pay extra attention to "signals" that come from your professor in the one or two classes before a test.* Professors usually make a point of not only reminding their students that a test is coming up, but also of the chapters that the test is based on as well as some of highlights. They'll also remind students about the type of test they can expect: whether it will be a long-answer, short-answer, essay-type, multiple-choice, or even a combination format.

- *Word process or type up your notes.* Besides being an excellent way to review, edit, and generally "weed through" your notes, this is another important opportunity to reinforce your learning. If you can take the time to do this nightly when you get home—or at least on a weekly basis over the weekend— you'll be creating a streamlined version of your notes, your "course synopsis." You can also use these word processed versions as handy summaries from which to study.

- *Use the "buddy system" to rehearse main points for a test.* Working with another student for a few study sessions, start by writing down some key concepts in point form on index cards. Then use the cards to give short "lectures" to the other student on those points; when you're finished, the other student then takes a turn and explains other course concepts while you listen. There are several advantages to this: the student who's lecturing learns through presenting the ideas and from the feedback of the listener; the listening student also learns through hearing the ideas and judging the presentation. Doing this even a few times greatly increases your learning level through reinforcement.

- *Go over all review materials your teacher hands out.* Teachers and professors will often pass out summary sheets, review questions, or highlight points to the class before a text or exam. Treat these seriously as "arrows" pointing you in the direction of which specifics you absolutely need to cover. If you don't get these from the teacher, make up your own.

- *Do chapter reviews on a daily and weekly basis.* The saying "a penny saved is a penny earned" could be rewritten here to read "a chapter reviewed is a chapter learned"—such is the power of frequent and regular reviewing. Studies have shown that seeing something once or twice after the original viewing greatly increases our ability to retain and remember it. Do a quick review of chapter highlights at the end of each day, and then spend at least a half hour to an hour on the weekend reviewing those same chapters in more detail. Think about it: if advertising worked perfectly the first time we saw it, why would we see any commercial more than once?

- *It doesn't matter what you start to study, as long as you start to study.* Sometimes, even with all the best intentions, it's hard to get going. If starting with your hardest subject or material (as we discussed earlier) doesn't work, then just plunge right in with anything. Or if working in a chronological or linear way from start to finish isn't working for you, don't try to force it. If you're stuck, just start with whatever detail or idea catches your eye or interests you in any way. Once you get rolling, the momentum will begin to build and you'll find yourself including whatever it is you need to cover.

- *Learn how to highlight effectively.* When reviewing your notes, you might be tempted to highlight more than you really need to. It's happened more than once that I've walked through a class during an open-book test and seen the pages of some student's textbook highlighted completely from top to bottom! The point of this is clear: if you highlight everything, you end up highlighting nothing!

- *Highlight only a few key words or phrases on any page*—that way, you can isolate just what's important while understanding that the rest of what's on the page is only explanatory or supporting detail.

- *Give yourself enough time to get the job done properly.* Trying to fit a month's worth of material into one evening's study session is unrealistic. Map out a reasonable timeframe for what it is you need to cover and do it in "bits and bites" over a period of time. For instance, that month's worth of material would be better subdivided over four weeks—or even one week if necessary.

- *Use a "game show" approach to memorize facts and details.* Write out index cards with questions about important dates, places and names of people that need to be memorized. Ask yourself (and answer) these questions at the beginning of a study session and keep track of your score. Then, at the end of that session, ask yourself those same questions again to see how much you remembered and compare your scores. When you repeat this exercise over time, your scores from the ends of your study sessions should gradually improve.

- *Make study checklists for each of your courses.* These lists should contain all of the important dates, tasks, assignments, and skills you need for that course. As well, be sure to include course concepts, ideas, highlights, theories, definitions, and formulas. These checklists will help you create a concrete structure for the substance of a course and give you a clear sign as to what is actually necessary to learn. Not having a checklist is much like going to shop at a grocery store without having a list of what you need—you'd end up guessing at and likely forgetting most of what you came for.

- *Make an appointment to see your instructor or professor about the test.* Unfortunately, students hardly ever do this. Many may be intimidated by the thought of speaking to the professor while it may not occur to others that the person who teaches the course would be an obvious source of information about it. I have always welcomed students coming to see me about upcoming tests or exams and, while I won't tell them what the specific questions will be, I will be open about which topics to focus on, the types of questions to expect (long- or short-answer), and strategies for reviewing. Overcome your shyness or reluctance and speak to your teachers—it's a great way to gain an edge.

- *Take the night off before a test or exam.* If you've prepared diligently and regularly, it makes sense to say that you can reward yourself the night before with a movie or a quiet evening "away from the books." This not only relieves stress, but it also removes your focus from course content—the result should be that your focus is keener when you need it the following morning.

- *Cram the night before a test or exam.* If you haven't prepared (as in the previous point) or if you just don't feel comfortable taking time away from even last-minute studying, then doing some "creative cramming" isn't necessarily a bad thing. Use this valuable time to focus on sections that you think are the most relevant, skim important parts of the text, make cue cards with key concepts, or memorize by audibly repeating key information. You won't learn the whole course in an evening, but highlighting important material can create a "comfort zone" for many students.

- *Look for copies of old tests or exams.* You may know students who previously took the course you're in and they could still have copies of old tests; you might find some of these tests in the library or the student association; or, you can ask the professor if any of these are available to students. In all cases, make sure that your studying from old tests is in line with academic or department policy. Also, be careful not to get too focused on these tests or exams—use them only as a rough guideline because you can be tripped up if you think that those exact questions will be on your test. Professors routinely change their tests from semester to semester so don't make false assumptions about test questions.

These points are useful ideas for creating a study plan, a structure that can give you strong sense of taking control over a test or exam. As with the other aspects of short-term study strategies we've looked at, the same logic applies here: however you can, try to anticipate or forecast the unknown (the test). Because the consequence of failing to do so is to simply walk into the test room unprepared, wildly guess at answers or leave them out entirely, and then be disappointed with the poor results. I've seen students do both, and

I can honestly say, that the ones who had a plan were happier with what they achieved.

HOW DO YOU DEAL WITH TEST STRESS?

Knowing how to deal with the stress or anxiety that comes from facing a test or exam is crucial to your success.

It's one thing to take in all of these tips and techniques and use them to get better marks; but even so it's still human nature to be stressed about a test or exam, which are really situations that can put pressure on you.

In a general sense, the most helpful things you can do to help yourself involve preparation and repetition. In almost all cases, students who are well prepared for a test or exam experience less stress than those who aren't. Similarly, those who prepare effectively time after time find themselves more in control of their circumstances and therefore feel less anxiety as well.

All of the following tips are designed to reduce stress and anxiety either before or during a test. In addition, all of them should become part of your preparation strategy and all are techniques that you should successfully repeat:

- *Start your study routine early enough, usually one week before a test or exam.* If you're studying for a test, often 1 hour per night is enough; if it's a mid-term or final exam, spend 2 hours a night every night. Remember that you are only either controlled by these situations—or are in control of them. I've heard students say "Poor me, I know I won't do well because I just didn't study," while I've seen others leave the exam room quietly confident because they know they did what they needed to do.

- *Communicate with your classmates and friends.* Talking to your fellow students is a good way to get a sense of their strategies and find out if there's more you should be doing or if you're far ahead of others. You could also compare notes or think of probable test questions together. And, while talking to your friends who aren't taking that course isn't helpful in the same way, it can be a positive way to at least talk out your feelings and perhaps shed some new light on your situation.

- *Practice writing an "imaginary" test.* As you're going through your notes, think of possible questions that could be asked about the material you're studying. Write down a few of these and then look back at the parts of your notes that you highlighted or that the professor drew special attention to. If you can connect your questions to these highlights, then you're probably on the right track as far as doing some creative predicting goes.

- *Learn some calming techniques.* If you're hit by test anxiety while studying, you can lessen the strain simply by switching study activities regularly; staying with mostly one type of activity for too long a time can cause you to lose focus which, in turn, can lead to increased apprehension. You can also do some deep breathing or muscle relaxing exercises for a few minutes to help you remain clam. Try to close your eyes, relax your shoulders, and slowly take a few deep breaths. Or do a muscle "tensing and relaxing" routine in which you consciously tighten and relax any part of your body that feels overly stressed. You can practice a sequence from your feet upwards or from your head downwards, going through the muscle groups. Another relaxation strategy involves visualizing your success—try to "see" yourself actually getting back your test with a good mark, or imagine a picture of yourself writing the exam calmly and confidently. Use whichever of these techniques works best for you and make it a part of your test preparation.

- *Try some light exercises to lower tension.* During study breaks, take a few minutes to do a few leg lifts, sit-ups, squats, or push-ups. The idea here is not to work up a sweat exercising, but rather to shift your focus from mental to physical for a short time. While this is easier to do when you're studying at home, you can always do some short, quick exercises on the morning or afternoon before you leave to write a test.

- *Get sufficient rest.* You already know how many hours of sleep you need in order to feel rested under normal circumstances, so why would you think it makes any sense to say you can perform just as well on less sleep in pressure situations? "Burning the midnight oil" is often less a sign of dedication than it is of desperation. Students who fall asleep in class or those who stay up late to cram are doing themselves a double disservice—they're increasing the pressure on themselves at the same time they're decreasing their rest level. If you follow a study strategy, you should still be able to get the rest you require to do well.

- *Conduct yourself like a confident achiever.* This fits into the "walk the walk" and "talk the talk" mindset—which has everything to do with adopting the behavior and posture of successful and confident students. Walk into the test room confidently and with good posture—creating a physical image of yourself as successful can go a long way to calm inner uncertainties about your performance.

There's a mild form of stress that can be called "good stress" when you're studying for an exam or are actually sitting down to write one. This is the kind of low level or expectant anxiety that causes a "butterflies in the stomach" feeling that comes from facing the unknown and it's a normal feeling that almost everyone experiences. This type of test stress isn't necessarily a bad thing—indeed, it can actually heighten your senses and cause you to focus and concentrate more effectively.

The other kind of stress, though, the overwhelming "kick in the stomach" variety, is the one you definitely want to avoid. And it's that stress that these tips are meant to help you deal with.

DO YOU TEND TO PROCRASTINATE?

Procrastination is the thief of time.

He or she who hesitates is lost.

Don't put off till tomorrow what you can do today.

These sayings show just how vulnerable people are to delaying what needs to be done. And students are no different than anyone else.

Watching a favorite TV show, spending time in the student pub, or shopping with friends are all more attractive and easier to do than "hitting the books." Almost every student will procrastinate once in a while—they'll put off tackling that assignment or delay studying for a test till the very last minute.

It's only when procrastination becomes a habit, though, that it really becomes a problem. When you dodge that much-needed study session time after time, what happens is that you end up putting more pressure on yourself by saving the inevitable till the last minute. Multiply this by the number of courses you're taking and then by the number of semesters in your program, and you end up with a recipe for disaster.

The interesting thing about procrastination is this: it can harm you only if you let it harm you. Because procrastination works only through passivity—that is, it can affect you only if you do nothing—then your simply choosing to act at the right time means that you can take away its power.

As we saw in the Part 3 section "You Decide," when you make a conscious decision to exercise your choice and will, there's much you can do to determine the positive outcome of your behavior. It's the same here. Your choosing to study rather than to put it off is entirely your choice—and you're the only one who can make it.

Take this short "procrastination test" to see how you do (here's a tip: don't put it off!)

PROCRASTINATION TEST

Use this rating to answer the following 5 questions:

> 5 = Strongly Agree
> 4 = Agree
> 3 = Don't Know
> 2 = Disagree
> 1 = Strongly Disagree

1. I'd rather spend time with my friends than studying.   *1 2 3 4 5*

2. I put off studying as long as I possibly can.   *1 2 3 4 5*

3. I let things interfere with my study time.   *1 2 3 4 5*

4. I have to pressure myself to get my work done.   *1 2 3 4 5*

5. I look for reasons to put off doing what I have to.   *1 2 3 4 5*

Scoring—add up your ratings to get a score

5-10   You're determined to make the best use of your time. You don't let things get in the way of what you need to accomplish.

10-20 You could be more focused on using your time effectively, but you're not in the "danger zone" of letting events control you.

20-25 You are in serious danger of allowing valuable study time to slip away.

Whichever range applies to you, most students can benefit from some "fine tuning" about how they handle their tendency to procrastinate. Look at the following tips on how to avoid letting procrastination get the better of you:

- *Adopt a personal slogan for yourself like, "Better now than later."* For most students, it's unfortunately the other way around, but in this case it's better to be the exception than the rule. Marketing companies spend millions of dollars creating slogans for corporations (Nike's "Just do it," McDonald's "You deserve a break today"), so why not take a page from their book and make one up for yourself? It may seem silly at first, but it can be an effective way of making your long-term goals a part of your everyday mindset.

- *Treat your studies as though they were your 9-5 job.* You wouldn't think of procrastinating at your actual job at the risk of being reprimanded or fired, so why not think in the same terms to help yourself get serious about your studies? Of course you're not going to be "fired" for not studying, but the consequences of getting low marks or even failing are certainly serious enough.

- *Tackle the task at hand immediately.* When you recall that you really have only two choices—to do it now or later—why not consciously choose the one with the payoff that leads to top marks? Besides, just starting to study increases the likelihood of your finishing the task, whereas if you never start you can be sure you'll never finish it.

- *Practice "reverse procrastination."* List the things that can prevent you from getting to your studies now—going to a movie, sitting at an outdoor patio, window shopping—and treat them instead as your later bonus for getting at your work now. By doing this, you're reversing their status from "impediment" to studying to "reward" for studying.

- *Think of how good you'll feel when the test is over.* Focus on feelings like stress, tension, headaches, and the pressures that come from being in a "time sensitive" situation. By putting things off, you run the risk of experiencing these twice—when you're actually procrastinating before the test and when you realize the negative results of your delays. Conversely, by not putting things off, you can experience positive feelings of low stress and quiet confidence twice—once while preparing and the second time when you see the positive results.

- *Build small "achievement treats" into your study schedule.* Allow yourself rewards for getting your work done, anything from chocolates or snacks to a favorite TV show. These don't have to be big items or even time-consuming; they're just helpers to get yourself "over the hurdle" of actually bearing down on your studies.

- *Break down your task into manageable parts.* Sometimes procrastination can come from your simply feeling overwhelmed by the size of what it is you need to deal with. The effect of this can cause you to delay or to give up without even trying because you feel as though you'll never be able to handle it all. Dividing one chapter into three or four parts, for example, is a good way to reduce the size of what you previously saw as unmanageable.

- *Learn to just say "no" to friends and family who may present distractions.* This may seem difficult to do at first, but, when you remember that your studies are the means to the important goal of your career success, you'll be better able to handle these requests for your time. Also, remember that you're only postponing time with these important people in your life—it's all waiting for you when your test is over.

These are hints intended to help you get a "handle" on actually confronting the work you need to do at the time you need to do it. If you think of an image of an hourglass with the sand running from top to bottom, the sand that's running through is time going by—but when the bottom of the hourglass is full, that time is gone forever.

Think of that picture of the vanishing sand whenever you feel stuck by procrastination. If you lose that half-hour or that hour on that particular day, you'll never get it back to do what you should have done. Why not do the opposite instead? Why not "seize the day" by not procrastinating?

DO YOU HAVE A PREPARATION CHECKLIST?

Before you march into an exam room brimming with confidence because you've followed all of these suggestions, take a few moments to write out a checklist. This won't take long to do (you can use these questions for starters) and, once you have one, you can re-use it for all of your courses.

Your checklist is a brief summary of your study areas and acts as a reminder to ensure that you've covered everything. Think of it this way: if you're leaving for a long trip by car, what would your checklist look like to cover your vehicle (tires, oil, maintenance), your house (keys, light timers, newspaper delivery), your pets (dog kennel, budgie sitters, goldfish feeders), and emergency lists (numbers to call). It's quite likely that even to go on a trip with peace of mind, you'd end up making several long and thorough checklists.

The same is true here. In order to be truly ready, you still need to remind yourself to account for your level of preparation in all of these areas:

1) Have I read the portion of the textbook that the test will cover?
2) Have I read my notes thoroughly and identified the highlights?
3) Did I pay attention to small details as well as to larger concepts?
4) Did I leave enough time to study thoroughly?
5) Did I come up with potential test questions?
6) Have I memorized enough facts, dates and names?
7) Am I ready for long- and short-answer questions?
8) Do I feel rested or stressed?
9) Have I verbalized portions of the material as well as read them?
10) Have I used my study time effectively?
11) Did I use any review materials given by the professor?
12) Have I made use of old tests or exams?
13) Have I talked to my professor for any insights?
14) Have I typed up my study notes?
15) Do I know my strengths and weaknesses as a learner?
16) Have I practiced teaching some of the material to myself or to others?
17) Was it helpful to use the "buddy system" or a study group?
18) Have I visualized a successful outcome on my upcoming test?
19) Have I used calming techniques?
20) Is my confidence level high?

The more of these questions that you can answer "yes" to—and, even more to the point, a strong "yes"—the better off you are. You'll be set to walk into a test situation with the high level of confidence required to do the best you can and to get the highest mark you can.

But the degree to which you apply yourself to any of these strategies is entirely up to you. It's only you who can make the decision to learn how to study—to be as professional in achieving success as a student as an excellent athlete is in training "for the gold."

NOTES

NOTES

NOTES

NOTES

PART 6

HOW YOUR PROFESSOR SEES YOU

To see ourselves as others see us....

This is a tried and true saying that contains much wisdom. For, if we could judge how our actions or our words actually affect someone else, we might often save ourselves a lot of hurt or grief.

And, while this is abundantly true of life in general, it's equally true in the case of students and their professors. Think about this for a moment: if you could see yourself as your professor sees you, how much could you benefit from this awareness of your actions and words?

How your professor views you in class is critically important to your academic success and marks, but sometimes students don't think of this at all or take it seriously. But why should it be otherwise? Professors are only human beings, after all, and are just as sensitive to the good and bad qualities of others as anyone else is. The real difference between professors and anyone else, however, is that professors, like bosses at work, are in a position to make judgments based on students' behavior as well as on their marks.

The work relationship between bosses and their employees, however, isn't exactly the same as that between professors and their students. While bosses can fire employees for poor work habits like chronic lateness, professors can't actually "fire" their students. But they can take notice of behaviors, language and attitude that can play a part in how they treat and grade students.

It's entirely useful for students to consider these points as they apply to themselves. Why put yourself in a position where someone who holds a considerable amount of power over your academic career can judge your behavior negatively? Students have enough to worry about making sure that they learn the material well enough to do well, so why give these "external issues" the chance to pull your mark down?

WHAT NOT TO DO IN CLASS

Let's consider the list of negatives from the beginning of Part 3 to see how you could be hurt if these applied to you.

- *Students who don't attend classes or show up only when they feel like it.* Attendance is a hugely important feature of academic success. If you're not in class, it's a fair question to ask "How are you learning anything?" If classroom learning were simply a matter of students reading the textbook and being there only for tests, why not just change the format to a correspondence course and omit the classroom part of it? The simple truth here is that students who "exempt" themselves from regular classroom attendance are exempting themselves from the course—and all they usually ever attain is a bare pass at best. Attendance goes a long way to physically demonstrating to your professor your interest in the course— it's a lot like Woody Allen's quote that "Eighty percent of life is just showing up." I see a clear difference between the students who never miss a class and those who never make a class! I also take attendance on a sheet I pass out during each class, not so much to actually give marks for attendance, but more to create an "attendance pattern" for each student. That way, whenever it comes down to a situation where someone needs the benefit of the doubt with a borderline mark or a makeup test, I have something as tangible as that student's "record of interest" to refer to.

- *Students who don't buy the textbook.* As with the previous point, this is a clear signal to the professor that a student who doesn't make the effort to buy the required book isn't serious about doing well in the course. Without a textbook, a student has no other way of learning all the essential information in the course. Borrowing a book temporarily is not a solution because you have to return it, and assuming that you can get everything from the lectures is misguided—the lectures cover only a sampling of the highlights with the details left for students to read in the text. A student without a text is a lot like a carpenter without tools—you can't expect yourself to build very much. Sometimes students have said to me "The text is too expensive" while others try to photocopy parts or all of a text. The cost of a text is just part of the "cost of doing business," the cost of your education. All of these costs need to be factored in when a student makes a commitment to go to school; however, sometimes used texts are available at a reduced cost or you can apply for an emergency textbook loan from your department or the student association. And, as far as photocopying textbooks is concerned, that's the same as plagiarizing or stealing an author's ideas—it's a crime.

- *Students who sit at the back of a classroom so they can "hide."* While seating preferences are a matter of personal choice, it's still possible to see a pattern. When students are interested only in talking, "goofing off,' reading a newspaper, or doing homework for another course, they're most likely to sit at the back of the classroom. Perhaps they think I can't see them at a greater distance, or that there's some kind of "invisible shield" between us that's protecting them. Maybe they think that because they're so far away that I won't make the effort to speak to them. Whatever false logic motivates them, they're mistaken. From my vantage point at the front of the classroom, I certainly see what they're up to and I deal with their behavior. Of course, this is not to say that all students who sit at the back are like this. Interested students often sit at the back of the room and are not disruptive. In general, though, good students fit the other side of this pattern—they make every effort to sit closer to the front so they don't miss anything. It's here that they can catch all the details and make themselves available for discussion.

- *Students who don't prepare for class by doing the necessary reading or studying.* As we've seen earlier in this book, preparation is one of the keys to doing well. It's really impossible to imagine good results coming from no effort. Students who don't do the required reading or research are putting themselves at a noticeable disadvantage and can't logically expect to do well. This is much like going to a business meeting to decide on the next steps in a plant restructuring without knowing the details involved or being able to contribute to the discussion—there's simply nowhere to hide. In the same way, reading the textbook or studying for a test are the absolutely minimal requirements to understanding the material. The lecture or class discussion builds on this base of understanding—it's not intended to replace it. I've said before that students need to see class time as an opportunity to feature highlights or expand on concepts, not as the "baby first steps" of the process. Any student who isn't prepared by pre-reading is already at a disadvantage before even walking through the classroom door.

- *Students who casually stroll into class late.* Other than being a mark of rudeness, this kind of behavior is an indication of a student's negative attitude toward the course. Obviously, anyone can be late occasionally for a good reason. But when this becomes the norm rather than the exception, when it gets to be a regular habit, it says to the professor "I don't really care about your class." And it's an impossible sign for any professor to ignore or to feel good about.

- *Students who talk during a lecture or class activity.* This is another behavior that shows disrespect toward the professor and the learning environment. Students whose talking disrupts the flow of the lecture or class discussion are being noticed for the wrong reasons. They cause the professor to take valuable time away from the course content and create a negative impression. Even worse, they penalize the good students who are paying attention by breaking their concentration on the material. In my classes, students get clear guidelines about when talking is and isn't allowed—so when any of them cross the line they're already well aware of the boundaries. And while they may convey a poor impression of themselves, my main concern is always to protect the integrity of the learning environment and those students who are there to learn.

- *Students who hand in assignments late or not at all.* Once again, this is a matter of degree. Occasional "slippage" in promptly handing in a late assignment can happen to anyone. But it's the chronic offenders who try to take advantage of the system that create credibility problems for themselves. It's hard to believe someone who "cries wolf" by saying "I'm sorry, sir, but my essay is late" for the umpteenth time that semester. In past years, the popular excuse was usually "my dog ate my homework"; well, the computer must have devoured the dog because now what I hear is "my computer ate the file with my homework on it!" The best thing to do, if you have a legitimate reason for being late with an assignment, is to speak to the professor, give a valid reason for the lateness, be specific about how quickly you can submit it, and ask for indulgence with the assurance that it won't happen again. This kind of conduct conveys a sense of responsibility and conscientiousness on your part. But better yet, don't be late handing things in—professors will notice not only the laggards but also those students who make promptness their habit.

- *Students who don't answer questions at all or who are sarcastic in their replies.* This is not to say that all students are extroverts who jump into a question session or enjoy being in the thick of classroom debate. But if you're not comfortable speaking up about some of the issues that are addressed during the semester, you lose out on several levels. For one thing, it's hard for the professor to get a sense of how your mind works if your mouth doesn't; for another, these "idea scrums" offer an excellent opportunity to get your "two cents in," to actually be able to bring up something you disagree with or something that hasn't been mentioned. This doesn't mean that you have to say something in every class or that you should try to monopolize the discussion—but getting over your reluctance to speak is a useful way for your professor to assess your ability to deal with course ideas on a level other than by writing about them. If you've been doing well in the course anyway, your active participation can only help to boost your marks even more. So silence is not "golden" for students who don't take the opportunity to speak. And those whose only remarks are full of sarcasm or disdain are just hurting their chances of being taken seriously as students— the "negative image barometer" kicks in again.

- *Students who make "creative" excuses for their chronic absenteeism.* Students who miss many or most classes are obviously not interested enough in the course to make a serious effort to be there. But it often happens that these same students show up somewhere near the end pleading their case for themselves and begging for just enough marks to get through. And what creative excuses they come up with for not being there: "My grandmother has SLOWLY been dying"; "I've had a lot of appointments with my parole officer"; "I had to leave the country unexpectedly"; "My money ran out so I had to get a full-time job for the last two months"; "My daycare vanished so I had to stay home with my kids"; "My car was stolen so I had to look for it"; "My wife is pregnant and I had to stay home"; "I'm cutting a CD with my band and lost track of time." To be sure, whenever an assignment is due, I never hear about as many scourges of family deaths, plagues of personal illnesses, and calamities involving technological breakdowns as I do then. If these students spent their energy and creativity on their attendance and course work rather than on coming up with such excuses, they'd be much better off—much like the many students who aren't absent and therefore don't need excuses.

- *Students who don't take notes or keep a record of course highlights.* Most of the time these are the same students who come up short in these previous categories. This is just another way of not being involved in the objectives of the course and it's also easy to spot. If students don't take good notes how can they hope to remember everything that was discussed over the term? And, when they combine this omission with not having a textbook, how is it possible that they would understand any of the course material? In Part 4, I emphasized the central importance of notes and it looked like this: no notes equals no medium-term study strategy. It's no accident that students who don't take notes are only taking up space in the classroom—it's virtually impossible to remember anything significant about the course without some record. Students who do take notes, however, are also easy to spot and easy to remember. Their actions send out the signal that they're alert to what's being said and that they're making an effort to capture the main ideas.

- *Students who convey a general attitude of boredom, disdain, or indifference.* This student is usually some mixture of the preceding categories. Students who show by their negative actions or by their omission of positive ones that their attitude is one of disregard for the course are at best on a kind of passive "cruise control" or at worst actually undermining and subversive. There is a local police force that carries the motto "deeds speak" on their police cars—well, the actions of these types of students also speak by their deeds and for the most part they don't have anything worthwhile to say. They're the complete opposite of those other students who are just as easy to spot—the ones who are committed to their studies and behave that way.

These behaviors and attitudes describe students who disadvantage themselves, who are "their own worst enemy." They see themselves as "a little too cool for school" and I'm often at a loss to explain why they would be there at all. The most I can do is hold them accountable for their behavior and try to contain it so that it doesn't hurt students who are really trying to learn.

There are two things that usually happen with students like these: one, by my holding them accountable and by putting them in classroom situations where they respond to peer pressure, some of them actually make an honest effort or even pass; two, the really "hard cases," the ones with the dyed-in-the-wool "why bother?" attitude, generally give up and drop out.

I feel sorry for these students, but I don't forget that my first priority is to maintain a positive learning environment for the class as a whole, and especially for those students who are there to learn.

The thing that you can learn from all of this is to not let yourself slip into these categories because, without a doubt, your professor won't be fooled by these behaviors either. And the only thing you'll succeed in doing is keeping yourself from getting the top marks.

HOW TO DEAL WITH YOUR PROFESSORS

There are always two sides to a coin—and two sides to students. As I said earlier at the start of Part 3, the students we've just discussed are in the minority. Most students are serious about their studies—or trying to be—and are always looking for good advice about how to improve. They do everything they can to nurture a "culture of learning" in themselves and they're open to whatever will help them achieve that.

These are students who see their studies in a positive light, and who understand that their professor plays a key role in the learning process. This role goes beyond simply being the person who doles out marks to a more enlarged view that sees the professor as a resource and an ally in your own learning.

Once you start to see your professor (in any course) as the person you *can* and *should* rely on to help you learn, you can benefit in a number of ways.

- *Be seen and be heard.* As we've seen, professors make

judgments based on negatives—but they also make them on positives. When you're in class regularly and when you make comments and ask questions, your professor actually sees the high degree of your involvement and can easily make a positive assessment of it. These are tangible indicators that say "I've read the material and I'm listening to the discussion—even to the point where I have to ask about it!" Professors need to be able to measure the extent to which you're interested in and engaged by the ideas in the course; these kinds of physical expressions of your interest give the professor more to go on. (Of course, I don't mean asking "goofy" questions or speaking just to hear the sound of your own voice). Apart from your learning the material that much better, there can be an advantage for you in marks: if your mark falls on the borderline between a B and a B+ the professor can use the valuable assessment of your classroom involvement to correctly justify giving you the higher mark.

- *Take a leadership role in class group work.* Whenever there's an opportunity for you to be part of a group exercise in class, don't just sit there and say nothing. Professors walk around and observe the interaction (or lack of it) within the groups and make similar judgments as those in the previous point. Without "bullying" your way into a leadership role in your group, find a tactful way to give some guidance to the discussion: offer to be the group "secretary" by taking notes; ask some focus questions of the group members; be the one who puts the group's points on a flipchart sheet. The learning benefit for you is the development of your group skills that will help you when you're in the work world. The benefit in terms of marks is that your professor has another positive example of your abilities in action.

- *When in doubt, check it out.* Sometimes you'll miss hearing the due date for an assignment or a test. When that occurs, don't just sit there without saying anything. Speak up and ask. If it's disruptive to do so at that point in class, speak to the professor during the break or after the class. Similarly, if you didn't catch all of the requirements of a particular assignment, check with the professor. Besides benefiting from taking a proactive approach to your task, this behavior conveys your sense of responsibility to your professor. Students themselves are the only losers when they miss valuable information; it happens too many times that they let things go by when all they had to do was ask.

- *Don't treat your professor as someone who's unapproachable.* This point follows from the previous one. It's one thing to recommend that you speak to your professor—it's another to assume that you're not shy, uncertain or even afraid to do so. But you shouldn't feel this way at all—even though too many students do. Students need to see the professor as the "guide" for that course, the person who gives information, instructions, directions and who tests for knowledge. Why wouldn't you want to consult such a person when you need to? If you saw your bank manager for a loan, you'd need to have a thorough discussion and probably ask necessary questions; the same is true if you saw a doctor at a hospital or spoke to a police officer at an accident scene. These are all people whose role it is to guide you through a specific process, and it's the same with your professor. So "don't hold back—just go up and ask" should be your attitude in this situation. And one more thing: don't treat your professor like a delicate, porcelain figurine that would crack if you opened your mouth—we're all used to discussions and questions and would actually prefer to get them than not.

- *Make an appointment to speak to your professor about an assignment.* Most students go through their entire time at college or university without ever making an appointment to speak to their professor. This is an astonishing reality. I'm sure it's safe to say this wouldn't be the case with your new car—every squeak, groan, or grind it made would likely send you to the dealership to speak to a service manager. So why is it different with your professor? If you see value in the fact that you're paying for your education and in the effort you're making, what's wrong with checking things out with the person in charge? It certainly can't be that students are afraid to talk—every time I pass the campus pub I have ample proof of that! So make an appointment for 10 or 20 minutes to go over that returned assignment to find out where you went wrong and what you need to do to improve the next time. I know that when I went through university, my professors became quite used to seeing me for a Q&A when I needed my questions answered—that's when I started to think in terms of the motto, "If you don't ask, you'll never know." If it's a small matter and you don't need an appointment, think of asking about it briefly before or after a class or during a break.

- *Be sure to always do homework and hand in assignments on time.* Again, these actions demonstrate responsible and punctual behavior. Your professor keeps records of the class's marks and completed assignments and knows exactly at any given moment which students have handed in everything and which have "holes" or empty spaces next to their names. Just one look at this mark sheet can tell the whole story as to who is taking things seriously and who isn't. Why put yourself on the wrong side of the "ledger" when you don't have to?

- *Understand the difference between the one and the many in a classroom environment.* In any given classroom or lecture hall you're ever in, there are essentially two "groups" of people—the professor and the class. The professor is the single person (the one) and the class is, of course, made up of a number of students (the many). As the leader of the class, the professor obviously has to "perform," to deliver the course and to manage the class. There's no escaping the fact that the professor has to be the active element in the class, and that leaves the body of students as the passive element, listening and taking in information. And it's here that the problem arises: because students see themselves as part of a larger group, they can become quite passive when they shouldn't be. Whether it's out of shyness or fear of speaking in front of a group, or thinking that "Maybe someone else will ask the question that I want to ask," students too often blend into the group rather than stand out in front of it. You need to be able to separate yourself enough from "the many" and think: "I know I'm part of a group, but I'm really one individual, and I need to get my question answered." This isn't always easy to do but it's an important step in taking control of your education. Don't let your perception hold you back.

- *Practice politeness with your professor and classmates.* This is more than a tip of the hat to The Golden Rule. It's apparent to almost everyone that we can only expect to be treated in the way we treat others. But this is also one more thing that registers with your professor. When you're polite and courteous to your colleagues and professor, you increase your stature as a respectful student, and that's noticed in a positive way. Sometimes cynical students sneer at this as a way of "sucking up" to gain extra marks; but there's a big difference between empty fawning and genuine respect for others and it's not that hard to detect. And there's an added benefit from behaving politely that shouldn't be missed—when you cultivate an environment of courtesy and respect in the classroom, it becomes natural for you to carry that behavior into your job or career, where your livelihood will depend to a great extent on how well you get along with others.

- *Don't mistake criticism of your work as criticism of you.* It's happened many times that students interpret a professor's comments on an assignment or a low mark as personal criticism of themselves: "I only got a D so that means he doesn't like me!" is one version; "I didn't pass so she must think I'm stupid!" is another. Nothing could be further from the truth. Professors evaluate the written work on a page or the expression of ideas in an oral presentation—not the student as a person. When you think about it, even the behaviors we've been discussing are "separate" from you as a person (the behaviors are what you do, while the person is who you are).   Students, therefore, need to work hard to detach comments on or criticism of their work as a personalized commentary of them. Focus more on how you express your thoughts, ideas, and concepts—that's what the professor is watching for.

- *Resist negative peer pressure.* If you find that other students you associate with in any of your classes don't share your commitment to studying, make every effort to avoid them. They may call themselves your "friends," but, if they interfere with your studies or affect your attitude the wrong way, it's up to you to be firm and stop "hanging out" with them. Look at it this way: if your "buddies" aren't going to help you earn your pay at your job, then why would you expect them to help you get top marks if they get in the way of your studies? Remember that you have the ability to choose your friends— so don't pick the negative ones. Instead, spend time with students who really are interested in learning—it's not that hard to make the switch. That old saying "You can tell a lot about someone by who their friends are" is a good thing to keep in mind.

- *Remember to remember.* This isn't meant to sound mysterious; it's just an encouragement for you to remember these tips, hints, techniques and strategies. As well, on a regular basis, remind yourself of your career goals and of the sacrifices you're making. Think too of how prepared you are, of your conduct in class, and about how you relate to your professor and classmates. If you try to recall these important details frequently, you're reinforcing a positive attitude and building a supportive mindset to get you through the tough times.

Professors didn't get to where they are overnight. They studied long and hard to arrive at their position, but their struggles are based on a "labor of love." I don't really know any professors who are teaching for a reason other than the fact that they love to learn and they love to teach.

It's helpful that students understand this side of professors, and not simply see them as "information dispensers." In the very best sense, professors are in front of the class as role models for learning. Their purpose is to convey the "joy of learning" and the "joy of teaching," and the highest compliment that any students could ever pay professors is to become as engaged in and excited about that process as they are.

I personally have a long list of names of my own professors who "led by example." I would watch their enthusiasm during class debates, try to catch their passion for their subject, and wonder at their total commitment to ideas and learning. And, over my own years as a professor, I too have tried to reflect those same values to the thousands of students I've taught.

When students know these things about their own professors, they'll be that much closer to what truly goes on in a classroom: you'll understand the truth that exists at the core of every course you ever sit in—that professors are always looking for students who honestly and eagerly want to learn. They're looking for students who value what they value. They're looking for students who are like themselves.

If you too can be in that classroom for these genuine reasons and if your actions and words convey your sense of purpose, then it's much more likely that your professor will recognize you as one of those students.

WHOSE COURSES ARE THEY ANYWAY?

It's up to you, then, to be excited about learning and to make the effort required to put these strategies into practice. These are your courses and you're the only one who can make the decisions necessary to get everything worthwhile out of them. Recall the section "You Decide" in Part 3 when we discussed the motivation necessary to make a genuine commitment to learning. That same sense of responsibility is actually what you need throughout the course of your studies, each and every day. Is it easy? No. Is it worthwhile? Again, only you can decide.

Some students simply won't make the effort. Others think that they can "breeze through" without lifting a finger. But as we've seen throughout this book, the opposite is the reality—desire, dedication, and drive are the "3 D's" essential to your doing well.

There's an old baseball saying that goes like this: "The further away you get from the dirt, the easier the game is." To the spectators in the stands, in the press box, and watching on TV, the game looks fairly easy. They might say "That pitch looked easy enough to hit!" or "Even I could have made that catch!"

There are also students "in the stands" of the classroom, looking down on the course, on the professor, and on the work being done. To them, the "game looks easy"—they're the spectators. They show up only when they feel like it, they don't read the text or take notes, and they don't study. They're just "watching" the course from somewhere up there, not actually involved.

There are other students, though, the "players" who do get involved. These are the ones who know why they're there, who make an effort, and who want the rewards. They ask questions, read and prepare, and put their study plan into action. And they're the "winners" on the "learning team."

So if you're a student in high school, college or university, and want to get the best from your time there, you'll be a player, not a spectator. You'll take responsibility and be accountable to yourself. It's then you'll know the meaning of the expression, "If it is to be, it's up to me."

NOTES

NOTES

NOTES

NOTES

NOTES

PART 7

WHY WRITE TESTS?

More than once I've heard students say "Why do we have to write tests anyway?" or "Isn't there a better way for professors to find out what we know?"

Well, the answer is that there really isn't a better way. Certainly, there are other ways to find out what students know including essays, summaries, reports, and presentations, but the "test is one of the best." A test is particularly useful because it's a highly effective focusing device. It causes students to zero in on a certain chapter, to read, understand, and assimilate the material thoroughly, and then to *demonstrate their knowledge* in a test.

It's much the same as the case of those athletes we discussed earlier. All the training in the world doesn't let them see how they're really doing until they're "put on the spot" in competition. All their training is focused on improving themselves in trials, heats, and sprints to the point where they can actually compete.

For students, the class test is like the athlete's competition. There's certainly some amount of competing for marks (only a certain number of students get A's), but students' real competition is against themselves. The best students, like the best athletes, know that they want to do better than they did the last time. And they settle for nothing less than continual improvement.

So any pressure that good students feel before a test is only that which comes internally from themselves to do better. They've prepared, they're ready, and the test is a welcome opportunity to show to themselves that they're up to the task. This is entirely different from students who aren't prepared—for them, the test places an external pressure on them that only reveals their inadequacies.

If you've made the most of the tips, techniques, hints, and strategies in this book, there's no reason that you can't be a student who sees testing more as the natural part of your training than something meant to put pressure on you or to "trip you up."

THE DIFFERENCE BETWEEN TESTS AND EXAMS

Throughout this book I've referred more to tests than to exams, but they're essentially the same form of testing. The main differences lie in the amount and type of material covered, the level of formality, the frequency and the differences in weighting.

Tests are usually shorter than exams and they cover less material. A test can deal with only a chapter in the textbook or a limited number of ideas and concepts whereas an examination usually covers a half-semester's worth of material (the mid-term) or an entire semester's worth (the final). Also, in terms of type of material, tests often use shorter questions focusing more on details, facts and specifics, while exams favor long-answer types of questions focusing more on an overview of the course.

Level of formality and frequency are also important differences between tests and exams. Tests are less "formal" than exams in the sense that tests are shorter, they're given more frequently, and they're not as thorough as exams are. Exams, on the other hand, are longer than tests (and can take up to 3 hours to write), they're administered less frequently (usually only twice a semester), and cover more material (usually half of a course for a mid-term and the entire course for a final exam).

The final difference is in how tests and exams are weighted—that is, what percentage of the total course value they count for. Tests usually count for anywhere from 5-10% each while exams can make up anywhere from 20-30% (or more) of the entire value of a course. But the fact that a test isn't worth as much as an exam doesn't make it insignificant: when you consider that a course can perhaps have 4 tests per semester, those 4 tests can easily equal the value of one exam.

Knowing these differences between tests and exams is advantageous for several reasons: it tells you that you need to put a different amount of time into studying for each; that you need to cover the course material differently for each; and that you need to prepare for different kinds of questions (we'll look at some examples of the different types of questions in Part 10).

You obviously need to study longer for an exam just because it covers more. And, where you'll aim at studying more detail and specifics for a test, your focus on material for an exam will cover the broader concepts that connect the entire course. The same distinction applies to the questions: test questions are usually discrete, highly specific, and based on detail and fact, while exam questions are more likely to get you to relate the major concepts and ideas that span the whole course.

Once you get used to these differences, you'll make the slight shifts needed in your study routine for either a test or an exam. *What's important for you to see now, though, is that the tips, techniques, hints, and strategies in this book apply to both tests and exams.* And, while I mostly refer to "tests" when I'm describing these study techniques, those same techniques are equally valid when you study for exams.

WHAT TO DO BEFORE A TEST

Remember that everything in Parts 4 and 5 apply to your study strategy before a test. So your knowing those insights is a valuable start and you'll definitely want to use them. But there are also some things you need to think about in the "short term," on the day of the test itself.

- *Arrive at the test room early.* This may be too obvious a point to mention, but removing the unnecessary stress caused by non-issues like being stuck in traffic only makes sense. There's enough stress created by meaningful test conditions, so why create any more? Arriving early also gives you the peace of mind of knowing that you'll be able to use all of the allotted test time—I've seen too many students who show up late for a test and then "squirm" because they're short of time.

- *Find out beforehand what you're allowed to bring in with you.* Pencils, pens and erasers are usually allowed; texts, notes, calculators, and briefcases may or may not be; phones, pagers, and Palm Pilots either won't be or shouldn't be allowed in a test room. Find out about policy around water bottles—these days they're permissible even when other drinks or foodstuffs aren't.

- *Avoid anxiety-increasing situations.* Of course, it's natural that you'd talk to your classmates before an important test or exam, but be sure to avoid getting into discussions that only serve to make you more nervous. When others come up with questions like "How much did you study for this test?" or statements like "I'm so freaked out because I didn't study!" it's easy to feel that you didn't prepare enough either. The best thing to do here is to remove yourself so that you're not negatively affected: it might be time to rummage through your backpack or to go to the washroom.

- *Use calming techniques.* Short of turning yourself into a yoga expert, use some of the calming techniques from Part 5 to lower your physical stress and help yourself focus. Before you open your exam, close your eyes, relax your shoulders, and take a few deep breaths. This might seem difficult to do (especially when everyone else is already flipping pages), but relaxing for even one or two minutes can help you focus more clearly.

- *Listen carefully to verbal instructions before the test begins.* These instructions can cover anything from how to ask to be excused to go to the washroom to typos on a certain page of the test. The more you know about the procedural issues regarding testing conditions, the sooner you'll start to feel in control of the test.

- *Recite an inspirational phrase any time you feel overwhelmed.* Whenever you feel that your emotions are taking over before or during a test, think of a motivational phrase or silently hum an upbeat piece of music to get back on track. Some students have told me they've repeated the slogan from *The Little Engine That Could*—"I think I can, I think I can"—while others have used the energetic rhythms of Rossini's *William Tell Overture*

(The Lone Ranger theme) to focus themselves.

- *Create a mental picture of your success.* Take a moment to visualize yourself having "aced" the test. Create a picture in your mind of yourself getting back the test with an A and glowing comments on it. This small but positive reinforcement can do much to give you a needed boost of confidence at a crucial time. And, if you've thoroughly prepared in the ways we've discussed, you wouldn't simply be fooling yourself with a "false" image of success.

WHAT TO DO DURING A TEST

OK, the big moment has arrived. This is what it's been all about. You're as ready as you'll ever be, and the test is about to start. What are the strategies that you need to know now to get you through as smoothly as possible?

- *Take off your watch and put it in front of you.* Use this as a visual reminder to divide your time among the test questions. When you actually see your watch in front of you (even if there's a clock in the room), you'll be prompted to pay more attention to using your time well.

- *Look over the entire test quickly before you start to write.* This simple exercise can give you a "reality check" of your situation; you'll either gain a sense of confidence because you're clear about the answers to the questions, or you'll know that you have your work cut out for you if you don't. Either way, you'll know immediately where you stand. As well, you'll have a good idea of which questions you'll need to spend more time on.

- *Read and understand the test questions.* Know absolutely clearly the requirements of each test question—then respond accordingly. For example, if a short-answer question calls only for highlights, then don't give details. Also, this will help you know precisely where you stand in terms of timelines, balancing values of different questions, and avoiding missing an important question.

- *Start with the answers to the questions you know best.* Tackle those answers first, then go to the ones you're less sure about. Chances are good that the thinking you do about the earlier answers will get you "into the flow" and remembering at least something about the harder ones. Use a colored marker to highlight the harder questions you can't answer right away so you can spot them easily when you come back to them.

- *Answer the shortest questions first.* In tests or exams that are made up of long- and short-answer questions, tackling the short-answer questions first helps you build your confidence as well as it gets you into the "flow" of starting to answer questions. Exam writing is like any other timed endeavor—once you're genuinely focused, all sorts of related information can readily come to you.

- *Identify key words to focus your response.* Words like "explain," discuss," "compare," "contrast," "analyze," "and "relate" are trigger words to help you focus your answer. They're like a signal pointing you in a particular direction—understanding what they're asking for will only make your job that much easier. Look at Part 10 for a full description of these test terms.

- *Create an outline for your answers.* Instead of writing blindly about your topic, take a few minutes to write an outline of key points that will focus it for you. Jotting down even a few words of phrases about the main ideas and putting them into a logical order can go a long way to giving a coherent shape to your developed answer in a short time.

- *Go for quality over quantity in your answers.* In a choice between long, rambling answers or shorter, concise ones, go for the latter. Professors care less about how much you have to say than about how focused your response is, so get to the main point in your answer as quickly as possible. And don't be distracted by students around you who write endlessly—chances are that they're not taking the time necessary to create an outline or to structure their answers.

- *Spend only the apportioned time on any one question.* For example, if it's 3 essay questions in a 3-hour exam, stick as rigorously as possible to one hour per question. Applying the law of averages, it's better to write 3 fairly good answers, than it is to write 2 great ones and miss one entirely.

- *Make sure that your writing is easy to read.* This may seem like a bit of a "selfish" point in favor of your marker, but when professors have to read hundreds of answers, even anything simple that you can do like this will make their job easier. Poorly written and messy handwriting might frustrate the person doing the marking and could end up lowering your mark.

- *Double-space your essay answers and write on only one side of the page.* This may seem like common sense, but there's a big difference for someone who's reading a cramped, single-spaced answer written on both sides of the page and one that leaves ample room and is less tedious to read. A bonus here is that the extra space you leave yourself can be used later if you want to add something before the time is up.

- *Don't be lulled by open-book tests.* Students can waste valuable time looking through texts in this kind of situation. If your test is open book, be sure to bring your book, but have the key points already highlighted with marker, post-its, tabs, paper clips, or crib sheets—search through the book only if you have to.

- *Techniques for multiple-choice questions.* Cover the answers to each question and try to think of the correct one before you read the choices. Dismiss the options that sound far-fetched or illogical immediately—then think harder about the one or two best choices. Mark your missed answers and come back to them later. If you have to make an "educated guess," then do so; you might get a mark for fluking a correct answer where you certainly won't get one for leaving the question blank.

- *How to deal with true/false questions.* Tackle these types of questions first to get them out of the way. Don't spend more time on these than you absolutely have to—they're usually not worth as much as other types of questions. The same applies to fill-in-the-blank-type questions.

- *Getting unstuck.* If you find that you "freeze up" or can't remember what you need to, try a simple technique like focusing on something similar or related to get you to the point you actually need. Jot down these similar terms or concepts in the margin to make these helpful points concrete.

- *Leave yourself time for a quick scan before the end.* Leave enough time—about 10-15 minutes on a 3-hour essay exam—for a scan of your answers. This lets you add something to an earlier question that you remembered while you were answering a later one as well as clean up a mistake or fill in a lapse. If you think about changing an answer, do so but be careful; in more cases than not, your first response is usually the correct one.

- *Say "good-bye" to your good effort.* There comes a point when you can't—or shouldn't—do any more. When you're satisfied with the effort you made and it's time to hand in your test or exam, just let it go. This time might come before everyone else is finished or right at the end of the available time. When you get to the point that you've answered and checked everything to your satisfaction, just realize that it's out of your hands and you've done the best you could. This brings a sense of closure to your experience and lets you acknowledge your effort.

If you remember to do these things during any test you write, you'll be well on your way to doing your best and to taking an important step toward improving your marks.

WHAT TO DO AFTER A TEST

There are some things you can do to make the most out of writing tests and exams and much of this has to do with what you do after you finish. Students mostly think "Well, it's over and that's it—I'll never have to look at that again!" and just walk away and try to forget about it. But there are a few things you can do to capitalize on the experience of any test you write, things that will help you do even better the next time.

Remember that athletes learn something from every competition they're in, and that they use that knowledge to gain an edge for the next one.

Here are some of those "post competition" exercises you should do:

- *Debriefing.* When you get home afterwards, sit in a quiet space for a while and assess your performance objectively in terms of "the big picture." Make sense of your experience by understanding its value to you mainly by how you handled the situation and what you learned about your ability to handle it. Ask some questions: "How do I feel I did?" and "Do I feel I did better than on my last test?" "Processing" your experience in this way will give you some perspective on all of your test experiences as a process rather than simply as a number of isolated experiences.

- *Reward yourself.* Regardless of how well you did on your test, you deserve to reward yourself in a positive way. Treat yourself to dinner, a movie or a gift. These don't have to be expensive rewards, but whatever you do serves as a tangible acknowledgement of your effort.

- *Recycle your effort.* If you've done well on a test or if you've improved your test-taking skills, "recycle" that effort by using it to help yourself on an upcoming test or exam. For example, if you know that the test you just wrote covered certain chapters that will also appear on the mid-term exam, you can use what you learned from the test (both knowledge and skill) when you write the exam. This will save you considerable effort at a later date.

- *Review sessions.* Many times professors will offer review sessions during which you can go over the test to find out what you did right and where you can improve. Apart from covering the right answers to the questions, these sessions will give you an idea of which concepts the professor thinks are important, how they relate to the course overall, and what kind of pattern you can detect for future tests.

- *Discuss the test with your professor.* We already discussed this point in Part 6, but if you have any concerns about why you received a lower mark than you expected, ask your professor. Too many students don't do this; they simply put their test aside and hope for better the next time. I've actually had students who consistently did well come to see me to find out about what they were doing right to make sure they were on the right track.

- *Keep a file of your tests.* It's a good tactic to keep a file of your tests for each of your courses to help you establish a pattern for future tests and, even more to the point, for mid-term and final exams. Let's say that you have 3 tests in a course before the mid-term exam—it's fairly safe to say that the questions on those tests will likely form the basis of the exam. So reviewing these tests is an effective way to predict the exam (there's never a guarantee that such patterns are foolproof, but the probabilities are high).

- *If we don't learn from our history, we're destined to repeat it.* This famous saying really sums up our learning and testing process. Namely, that if we never learn how to learn, how can we expect ourselves to improve? Don't be one of those students who file their returned tests in the circular file (the wastebasket). Keep looking for new ways to make good use of the testing experience so that when you hear the words "test" or "exam," your reaction is always a positive one because you now know what you're doing. When you get to this point, taking tests can even become "fun."

Doing well on tests matters as much to your perspective as it does to your marks. If you can see tests as (a) an inevitable part of your education and (b) a situation you can master by learning some skills, then you can step into a position of control over your situation.

Often, those students who "put down" tests or are afraid of them are really covering the fact that they feel like "victims," that they feel as though they are powerless. By learning and repeating the steps in this book, however, you're doing the most you can to make sure that you're not one of these. You're doing everything you can to take charge and, in doing so, are taking the responsibility for your own actions and your own success.

As we've seen, an athlete can have ability but still needs training and coaching to "get to the top." As a student, competing against yourself and others, you can use this book to give yourself the direction you need to get there too.

NOTES

NOTES

NOTES

NOTES

PART 8

WHERE TO GET HELP WITH STUDY TECHNIQUES

The goal of this book is to give you what you need to do well on tests and exams. The study techniques you've read about here didn't just come from nowhere—they're tried and true strategies that I've used for many years to help students learn. And they've been very successful. Thousands of students who applied these skills improved their marks dramatically.

My hope is that you are one of these students. It would be just great if your making the most out of these techniques caused you to become a better learner and to get the top marks.

However, if you feel that you need to find additional help, if you think you need a tutor or an ongoing support system, let me give you some ideas as to where to go:

- *Peer tutoring.* This kind of tutoring is usually offered for free at colleges and universities and it's meant to help students who are having difficulty with their study skills. Students can study one-on-one or in a lab with a tutor to prepare for assignments or exams. Most tutors are second- or third-year students who have already completed a training program and are paid by the college. Working with a peer tutor on either an occasional or regular basis can do a lot to help you hone your study techniques.

- *Writing workshops, study workshops, or learning centers.* As with peer tutoring, these workshops are designed to assist students who are looking for help with their writing or study skills. Students need to ask at their department to find out if such workshops are available. The difference between these and peer tutor situations is that writing and study workshops are staffed by graduate students in M.A. or Ph.D. programs or by professors.

- *Hire a tutor.* If you don't mind paying for the services of a tutor, you could use one on at least a short-term basis to learn some skills quickly. A quick search of the Yellow Pages, the classified ads, or on bulletin boards at school can give you some names to contact.

- *Student association or the library.* Check at either of these places for any kind of information you can get about help with studying—both are great referral sources. Also check posters for leads.

- *Bridging or upgrading courses.* For students who have been out of school for some time and are upgrading their skills, there are bridging (transitional) or upgrading courses available at most high schools, colleges and universities. Mature students, particularly, might need "brush up" study skill courses if they feel they've forgotten study techniques or weren't taught them in the first place. Do some research by phoning these places, getting some leads, and finding the skill level that's right for you.

- *Look through "learning network" publications or do an Internet search.* There are usually publications available at newsstands that feature learning or study skill training. Or you can conduct an Internet search for what's in your area by typing in either "study skills and (your city's name)" or "study skills links."

THE BELL CURVE AND WHAT IT MEANS TO YOU

There's a reality that all students should know about the minute they enter any class for the first time. And that reality is called "the bell curve."

Whether you know it or not, or whether you like it or not, it exists. Here's how it works: whenever a group of students makes up a new class at the start of a semester, that group fairly well divides itself into about three segments—a small "top" group, a large "middle" group, and a small "bottom" group.

What this means is that, by the end of the course, a small number of students will have achieved the high marks like A's (usually between 10-20%), a small number will have failed or gotten only D's (again about 10-20%), and the bulk of the remaining students will be in the middle range with either C's or B's (60-80%).

If you were to draw these ratios out on a horizontal axis of a graph, the line would be low on the left side, curve up in the middle, and then curve down low again on the right side—hence, the curved look of a "bell" (or it would resemble the silhouette of two shoulders and a head). This trend is commonly known as "the bell curve" and its application here comes from the fact that virtually every class of students divides itself along these lines.

It's important for you to know that the percentages referred to are not exact: one group of students might have a higher percentage of A's while another might have a higher percentage of D's, but in general these groupings are remarkably consistent from class to class and from semester to semester.

It's also important that you understand that professors don't necessarily "mark to the curve," or slot students into categories simply because they know that's how the numbers unfold. But, over my many years of teaching, I've seen the cold truth of the bell curve unfold time after time—and that really is how the numbers unfold.

How can you benefit from knowing this? In the simple sense that, if you know that statistically not everyone gets into that top bracket, you know that you have to do something to make sure that you're one of the ones who does.

You know from having read this book that you now have the tips, techniques, hints, and strategies at your disposal that you can use to make sure you get to where you want to be—in the "A group" of the bell curve.

APPEALING YOUR GRADE

If you ever find yourself failing a test or exam and feel that it was unfairly graded, you do have the recourse of appealing that grade. Consult the policies booklet or manual of your college or university to find out what the formal procedure is for an appeal, and you can always get help from such sources as your academic department, your student association or a student advocate.

Before you take this path, however, there are some reasonable steps you should take:

- *Talk to your professor.* Make an appointment to discuss your perception of how you did on the test or exam and find out exactly why you received a failure. If after you've discussed it you see that the F you received was not an unfair judgment, you obviously won't be taking things further. If you still feel that there was some unfairness in the grading, then you'll carry on—but it's always best to try to resolve these things at the discussion stage.

- *Find out if other students in your class also feel they were failed unfairly.* You'll have a stronger case for your claim if you can find other students who are also in your position. Make a list of their names and find out how many of them are committed to going through an informal appeals process.

- *Meet with your department chairperson in an attempt to resolve things.* Whether it's just you or a group of students, your next step after talking to your professor is to arrange an appointment with the chairperson of your department to discuss the situation. Your professor might be at this meeting, but it should be an attempt to find some common ground. A possible course of action could be to find a third party— another professor—to read and grade the tests in question.

- *View this process as a real but last resort.* If the meeting with the chairperson doesn't lead to a resolution, then it's on to the dean and so on up the academic hierarchy. This can be a long and tedious process and you'll need a "stick to it" mindset to get through it. Because of that you should look at formal appeals of marks as a last resort—always try to settle it at the early stages. But students need to know that there is a process in place to help them in cases where they genuinely believe that they've received an unjust failure.

WHY NOT CHEAT?

As I've seen over the years, cheating does unfortunately occur. A small percentage of students, for whatever reasons, have cheated on tests, assignments and exams. And a lot of them were caught.

When I look at a breakdown of which types of students most often cheat, I've noticed something interesting—that the students with the top marks are rarely the cheaters. In fact, it's usually not even the ones in the broad middle range that cheat either: cheaters have mostly been students whose marks are low, who are failing, and who are rarely in class.

That statistic tells me that the students who are prepared and who feel confident about their abilities are the ones who don't feel they need to resort to copying someone else's work.

That also tells me that what we've discussed in this book is of great value to every student, and especially to those who are more likely or more tempted to cheat. For if every student can master the study and test-writing skills essential to doing well, no one should ever feel a need to cheat.

For anyone who has ever cheated and for anyone who has ever thought about cheating, here's a brief primer on why that's not the best route to take:

- *Whose work are you copying from anyway?* Students who cheat are making one huge, false assumption: that the student they're copying from actually knows what the right answers are! What do they know about that person? Do they know, for instance, if that student is prepared, has studied, or has even read the book? And what if the student they're copying from is actually guessing? What they're doing is actually putting the outcome for their own success in the hands of a complete stranger, and all that this really does is expose their own level of desperation.

- *What happens if you get caught cheating?* The very least that happens is that you get an F for the test and the ripple effect of that mark will lower your total course mark. Your cheating also puts me on "red alert" for the next test (because I note the cheating incident in my files), so I'll be sure that you sit removed from anyone else from now on. Should you somehow manage to cheat again, you get another F, we discuss the situation in my office, and it's my discretion as to whether this is the point to involve the chairpersons of my department and of your department in a meeting. After a third incident, we skip the introductions and go straight to meetings that could result in your suspension or expulsion. So if students know that this is what awaits them, why would they even want to cheat?

- *Cheaters never prosper.* The self-fulfilling statement that "whatever goes around, comes around" is entirely applicable here. Students create their own "cycle of distress" when they adopt cheating as their approach to any or all tests because, if they don't get caught each and every time, they certainly increase the risk of being caught the more they cheat. And what this does is to raise their stress and anxiety to extremely high levels, leading to possible stress "burnout." They have to deal with the high probability that every time a test is returned it's going to have an F on it, and then multiply that anxiety by the total number of tests over 5 or 6 courses each semester— well, that kind of stress load can take its toll over 2 or 3 years.

- *The dangers of carrying negative behaviors into the workplace.* Cheating is unethical behavior that can become a habit and create a negative mindset. Once students start to rationalize this behavior as just a "temporary shortcut" and become used to it, there's a real danger that it becomes the norm rather than the exception. Then, when these same students graduate and get jobs, what's to stop them from carrying that same mindset into the workplace and cheating there?

- *Cheating literally robs you of the education you're in school to get.* You've paid a considerable amount of money for your education and you've put your career on hold—you've already made sacrifices just to walk in the door of your college or university, so why jeopardize that by cheating? You've found value in getting an education and by cheating all you do is rob yourself of that value. Think about it: if you're cheating, are you actually learning what you came to school for?

- *Don't cheat just because your friends are cheating.* As we've seen before, peer pressure can be a powerful influence. If most of the students in your class sit silently, chances are that you will too. If your friends decide that cheating is "cool" or an easy "short-cut," then the possibility that they'll tempt you is high. This is where you have to decide to separate yourself from them, even if it means finding new friends. If this isn't a simple decision for you to make, then reread all of these points about cheating.

STUDYING FOR ONLINE COURSES

There is a growing trend in post-secondary education toward distance education and online courses. Put simply, this refers to your ability to take a college or university course right from your computer at home without ever having to physically attend classes.

This works because you can enroll for such a course through the Internet just by accessing the website of a college or university, registering online, and then taking a course when it's offered in an upcoming semester. Of course, you need to have the necessary equipment to do this—including a sufficiently powerful computer, a phone, a modem, and a fax machine. It's also a good idea to do some research into this prospect by contacting the professor who teaches the course beforehand, by reading introductory information, and by talking to people who have taken these types of courses before.

Because you would be working on your own from your home, this can be an exciting option to traditional learning. Even though you might be at a great distance, you'd still be in close contact with the professor and your "classmates" through your Internet link. There's another benefit in the fact that you could do much of the course on your own time—even at 3 a.m. if need be—it's that flexible. If your learning style leans toward independent study, then online learning is a good choice for you.

There are some cautions that you need to factor in here though. First, online courses work best for students who can manage their time effectively. Students derive much motivation from attending classes regularly, and when that aspect of a course is taken away, they need to be extra vigilant about staying "on track" with a course. Second, online students need to be proficient with the technology and aware that technological breakdowns can occur during an online course. And third, online students need to be highly proactive by making sure that they get all their instructions clarified and questions answered because the immediacy of classroom contact is absent.

None of this is meant to discourage students from taking courses online. In fact, these types of courses are a growing trend in education and they can play an important role in students' learning. Find out about the possibility of your taking some courses online during your program, and at least consider using some to vary your type of instruction or to take during the summer to lighten your load in the fall.

NOTES

NOTES

NOTES

NOTES

PART 9

CAN STUDENTS' APPEARANCE AFFECT THEIR MARKS?

Given that we live in an age of tolerance where discrimination based on one's appearance is a no-no, is there even any point in asking if students' appearance can affect their marks?

For, as a natural part of any teaching day, in addition to all of the "average looking" students I see in jeans and T-shirts, I also see some sporting an "extreme look": tomahawk haircuts, pink hair, Goth outfits and makeup, tattoos, assorted body piercing, the 'hood gear, or the skinhead look. And then there are those under the age of 50!

Seriously, most of the time none of these features really causes professors today to even blink an eye—we've more or less seen it all. Whatever reasons students might have for adopting these styles is their business; what professors are really looking for are students who are seriously engaged in their studies—whatever they look like. I've had Goths get A's and "nerds" flunk, so "don't judge the book by the cover" is always my rule of thumb.

It can happen, however, that not all judgments appear obvious. It can happen that, while most of your professors won't connect your looks with your marks, someone might. You can go around thinking that you can "dress the way you like," but it would be wrong to assume that everyone will "like the way you dress." This judgment might be extremely subtle—getting a C instead of a B—but it can happen. And it could be based on your looks.

It's not impossible to imagine that this can occur. "Extreme teens" already get extra attention in shopping malls and movie theaters, so to say this kind of treatment can't happen is off base.

When students have talked to me about these things before, my advice has been to use some common sense. If your goal in school is to prepare for the world of work, think about dressing as you would for your job—not in shirts and ties or power suits, but in the casual wear of "dress down" Fridays. This just puts you a few steps ahead in the direction you're going anyway.

WHAT IF YOU DON'T LIKE YOUR PROFESSOR?

It's entirely possible that in the course of the 2, 3, or 4 years of your program you might run into a professor you don't like or can't get along with. What do you do then?

What I'm referring to here is not a minor situation where you can't hear the lecture from the back of the classroom or you can't read the comments on your returned assignment. In the one case, you can either move closer to the front or ask the professor to speak louder; in the other, you can ask for clarification.

The kind of situation I mean is more serious. An example can be like the one discussed previously where you felt you were unjustly failed. Another can be a situation where the professor delivers the content at a level that's inappropriate for that type of course and students aren't "getting it."

This second type of situation occurred to me when I took a Victorian Lit course as part of my Masters degree. About 15 students attended the first class and the professor started off well by giving an interesting overview and asking students what had attracted them to this particular course. Since everyone there had at least graduated from an undergrad program and was used to vigorous classroom discussion, the first hour went by quite nicely. Then, after the break, a new student showed up. It turned out that he was at the end of his

Ph.D. studies (thus, far beyond the rest of the class), and for the remaining class time he and the professor had a one-to-one chit-chat about details of authors and writing that the rest of us were just starting to learn about.

When the class was over, I walked out feeling angry and upset. I had no gripe with the professor as a person (I'd just met him and he seemed nice enough), but I was disturbed by his behavior when he ignored the rest of us after this new student "took over" his attention on a higher level. The professor should have taken control of the class and not made the rest of us feel like we were excluded.

I dropped the course the next day. I could have stayed and hoped that things would sort themselves out, and perhaps they might have. But I was also concerned that, if this happened once, it could happen again—and that I would be a victim of a mismanaged class. I was genuinely worried that my marks would suffer in these circumstances, so I had to accept responsibility for what I found myself in and act.

The good news is that this incident was a rare occurrence over many years. The vast majority of my professors were excellent teachers who treated their students with respect and always found ways to get the most out of our intellectual curiosity. And it will likely be that way with you.

My point is just that there may come a time when you have to make a tough and serious decision about what's right for you in a particular course. If that time comes, know that it's not a decision to be made lightly or to be used as an excuse—but rather a decision that you have to wisely assess and reluctantly take.

THE 8 GREAT WAYS TO STUDENT SUCCESS

As a professor who has seen thousands pass through my classroom over many years, I've had the incredible good fortune to meet many wonderful students. Some were younger, some older; some just starting out, some coming back; some single, some married with kids.

I have fond memories of these students, and, while I thought that I was the one teaching them at the front of the classroom, I discovered that a lot of the time I was actually the one learning from them.

I learned about commitment from Maria, a single mother who struggled to balance her children, her job, and her studies, but who won and graduated; I learned about personal sacrifice from Weng who left his wife and children behind in his home country to go to school and start a new life for them here; and I learned something about pushing past boundaries from John, a visually-impaired student who got higher marks than every sighted student in the class.

These and countless other students taught me the "nuts and bolts" of what it takes to succeed in school. They showed me the core qualities that students need in order to excel and I've written them down here as "The 8 Great Ways To Student Success."

1) *Pursue your bliss.* This is as straightforward as it gets. If you're not going after something that you really want to do—that you really enjoy—then why bother? If you've found the job or career that you have your heart set on and that you'll be doing for the rest of your life, then the chances are so much greater that you'll "move mountains" to get it. I once had a student in my class who was in her early 20s and had just quit her career as a fashion model. When I asked her why she'd left something that many people think is a glamorous life, she said "It wasn't me any more." She said that she wanted "food for her mind" and was happy to be in university.

2) *Stretch yourself.* Students sometimes "tighten up" in their minds about who they are and what they're capable of doing. They apply a kind of "mental straightjacket" to their aspirations and abilities and don't think "outside the box." Sometimes that tendency comes from within, sometimes from their peers or parents. Whatever the source, the consequences can be deadly to their inner growth. In my years of enrolling students, I'd be part of numerous conversations that went like this: Professor Bernie: "What's your program?" Student: "Business." Professor Bernie: "Which area—logistics, marketing?" Student: "Don't know—my parents suggested it." Professor Bernie: "Isn't that what you want?" Student: "No. I think I like Science, but they said I'd be better in Business." Professor Bernie: "Ouch!"

3) *Choose your attitude.* We choose our friends, we choose how to spend our time, and we choose our mate—so why can't we choose our attitude? I've seen students who complain, grumble, and criticize everything and their negative attitude literally paralyzes a class whenever they walk in. Yet that same

134

class behaves entirely differently when that student is absent. Why be that student? There's an old saying that says "attitude determines altitude." The higher, more upbeat, and positive your attitude is, the more opportunities open themselves up to you. We've all seen cases where someone walks into a room full of people and literally lights up the room with their presence, with their attitude. Try that test yourself: watch people's faces when you walk into a room. If the result isn't to your liking, boost your attitude and then see what happens.

4) *Look, listen, and learn.* There's much to be said for talking. Students like to talk and they spend a lot of time making their views known. And that's all right—they're developing, expressing their ideas to their fellow students and growing in the process. But there's also much to be said for the opposite— looking, listening and learning. A famous quote says, "We never learn a thing when we're talking." The power of actually listening intently to others is much underrated—too many people seem to be listening when all they're really doing is thinking about what they're going to say next. Here's an example of that power: my friend, Greg, was on a long plane ride and sat next to a businessman. The businessman talked non-stop during the several hours of the flight while Greg said hardly anything. As they got off the plane, the man shook Greg's hand and said he felt like he'd known Greg for his whole life!" It's amazing what saying nothing accomplished!

5) *Avoid energy" vampires".* There are people who give a lot and then there are those who take a lot. They take our time, our attention, and our energy. In short, they're a kind of drain on everything we try to accomplish. And they don't even have to come across as negative or nasty. In fact, they often seem nice and well intentioned: "Oh, gee, you're studying *again!* Why not give those heavy books a break, and we'll just catch that new movie!" If it's time for you to take a break in your routine, no problem. But, if this is a regular and recurring pattern, then you have a bona fide "vampire" draining your energy and time. Beware.

6) *You're not alone.* The great English poet, John Donne, is perhaps best known for his immortal lines: "No man is an island unto himself... Every man is part of the main." And the growth of our modern societies is proof of this—that which affects someone else somewhere else can easily affect us too. Knowing this, you should take some comfort in the fact that it's easier to share the things that bother you than it is to "go it

alone." It might not always seem simple to reach out to people either to unload or to listen to their troubles (guys usually find this extra difficult), but the rewards of sharing grief or joy with others are remarkable once you try it. A footnote here belongs to Simon and Garfunkle's song, *Bridge Over Troubled Water.*

7) *Contribute to the growth of others.* Helping others do better is really what teaching is all about. As a teacher, every time you help people improve their life situation or their character, you benefit at the same time by playing an important part in their growth. But this is also one of the most rewarding aspects of student life. How many times have I seen students help other students by explaining class notes, by helping with computer programs, by giving directions, or just by listening? The "rewards" may not seem obvious to the students doing the helping, but they're there if you look for them. For one thing, when you take the time to help another student, you can be sure that your effort and care are hugely appreciated. For another, by taking on the role of teacher, you grow by using the skills you've learned. It's a win-win situation.

8) *Enjoy the journey.* If there's one goal that runs through this book, it's the value of getting top marks in your courses. That's certainly a worthwhile goal in and of itself—the proof being the countless numbers of students over the years that have asked me for advice on how to achieve that. But there's something else of value in your getting an education that might be less obvious, but no less important. And that's the sheer pleasure of learning, of getting your education. How can you "enjoy the journey" of learning? By reading to improve your knowledge, by writing to express yourself better, by speaking to ask questions and debate issues, and by making friendships that last a lifetime. These are the daily activities that make up your education, but that also have their own worth and enjoyment. If it's true that "Life is what happens when you're making other plans," then it's also the case that "Learning is what happens when you go after the top marks." Have fun with it along the way.

A "GREAT BOOKS" READING LIST

As a parting "gift" to students when we finish a course, I like to give them something they can use to continue with their learning. That "something" is invariably a list of books that are a "great read." These are books that I've read, enjoyed and learned from, and my wish is that you will too.

Abbot, Edwin A. *Flatland*. New York: Dover Publications, 1952.

Asimov, Isaac. *I, Robot*. New York: Ballantine Books, 1987.

Beckett, Samuel. *Endgame*. London: Faber and Faber, 1972.

Beckett, Samuel. *Waiting for Godot*. New York: Grove Press, 1954.

Berger, John. *Art and Revolution*. New York: Pantheon Books, 1969.

Berger, John. *Ways of Seeing*. London: Penguin Books, 1986.

The Bhagavad Gita. Trans. Juan Mascaro. London: Penguin Books, 1972.

Borges, Jorge Luis. *Labyrinths*. New York: New Directions, 1964.

Camus, Albert. *The Fall*. London: Penguin Books, 1972.

Camus, Albert. *The Myth of Sisyphus & Other Essays*. New York: Vintage Books, 1955.

Camus, Albert. *The Outsider*. London: Penguin Books, 1972.

Clarke, Arthur C. *Childhood's End*. New York: Ballantine Books, 1988.

Cornford, F.M. *Plato's Theory of Knowledge*. London: Routledge & Kegan Paul, 1970.

Dickens, Charles. *Hard Times*. London: Everyman Books, 1969.

Evans-Wentz, W.Y., ed. *The Tibetan Book of the Dead*. London: Oxford Press, 1978.

Ewen, Stuart. *Captains of Consciousness: Advertising and the Social Roots of the Consumer Culture*. New York: McGraw-Hill, 1977.

Freud, Sigmund. *Totem and Taboo*. London: Routledge & Kegan Paul, 1975.

Golding, William. *Lord of the Flies*. London: Faber and Faber, 1969.

Herrigel, Eugen. *Zen in the Art of Archery*. New York: Vintage Books, 1971.

Hesse, Hermann. *Siddhartha*. New York: Bantam Books, 1974.

Holt, John. *How Children Fail*. New York: Dell Books, 1974.

Kosinski, Jerzy. *Being There*. New York: Bantam Books, 1970.

Kosinski, Jerzy. *The Devil Tree*. New York: Bantam Books, 1974.

Kosinski, Jerzy. *The Painted Bird*. New York: Bantam Books, 1979.

Laing, R.D. *The Politics of Experience and The Bird of Paradise*. London: Penguin Books, 1977.

Luxton, Meg and Harriet Rosenberg. *Through the Kitchen Window: The Politics of Home and Family*. Toronto: Garamond Press, 1986.

Merton, Thomas. *Zen and the Birds of Appetite*. New York: New Directions, 1968.

Novak, Michael. *Ascent of the Mountain, Flight of the Dove.* New York: Harper & Row. 1971.

Orwell, George. *Animal Farm.* New York: Signet, 1974.

Pacey, Arnold. *The Culture of Technology.* Cambridge: MIT Press, 1986.

Pirsig, Robert M. *Zen and the Art of Motorcycle Maintenance.* New York: Bantam Books, 1976.

Pirsig, Robert M. Lila: *An Inquiry into Morals.* New York: Bantam Books, 1991.

Plato. *The Republic of Plato.* Trans. F.M. Cornford. London: Oxford Press, 1976.

Sartre, Jean-Paul. *The Age of Reason.* London: Penguin Books, 1971.

Vonnegut, Jr., Kurt. Breakfast of Champions. New York: Dell Books, 1975.

Watts, Alan. *The Book: On the Taboo Against Knowing Who You Are.* New York: Vintage Books, 1972.

Watts, Alan. *Nature, Man and Woman.* London: Abacus, 1976.

Watts, Alan. *Psychotherapy: East & West.* New York: Pantheon Books, 1972.

Whitehead, Alfred North. *Science and the Modern World.* New York: The Free Press, 1969.

A FEW BONUS TIPS

Here's a "grab bag" of some bonus tips that you can apply as you continue to improve!

- *Look up the meanings of words.* Many times students encounter new words in their reading and don't bother to look them up. At most, they might guess at them based on the context of the sentence or paragraph. Don't let this be you. When you take the time to look up a word, you begin to "own" it. The more you do this with words, the more you expand your vocabulary and your ability to express yourself. Thoughtful and rich word usage is one of the hallmarks of educated people.

- *Use the 15-minute rule.* This is a simple, but effective "rule of adjustment." This is how is works: if you don't like doing something new or different, do it anyway. What you'll discover is that after about the first 15 minutes at it, you'll probably start to forget about how much you disliked it.

- *Revise thoroughly.* Don't ever hand in any assignment that contains errors or looks sloppy. Professors award and deduct marks not only for what you say, but also for how you say it and how it looks. Proofread carefully and often, correct all errors, and print your final copy to look neat and professional. Ignoring these points puts your work in a negative position before it's even read.

- *The "lurching express" model.* Students usually think they have to speed toward a deadline—but unfortunately leave the "speeding" part of their work to the last minute. It's much better, though, to do the opposite—start early and, instead of speeding, chip away at your work gradually in bits and bites over weeks and months. This way you kind of "lurch" toward your deadline, but arrive there with a more thoughtful result than that produced by the last-minute crowd. Remember, it was the turtle that won that race.

- *Knowledge put into action is power.* While most people are familiar with the expression "knowledge is power," this expanded version is even closer to the truth: "Knowledge put into action is power." I've referred to this idea in other parts of this book, but it's worth echoing once more. It means that it's what you do with what you know that's really important. A student might know all the right answers to the test questions, but if she doesn't write them down on the page, she'll get an F. Similarly, you might know all of the techniques we discussed in the book, but if you don't actually use them, can you expect to do better?

- *Take part in school life.* This is an often-overlooked dimension for many students. They arrive at school just before classes start and they leave when they're over. But in doing so they're missing a lot in terms of interaction with other students—and the library, computer rooms, sports facilities, student lounge, and campus pub and great places for this. There are also other meaningful things to do—work at the student association, run for election on the student council, work as a student advocate, write for the school newspaper, or be a peer tutor. When you involve yourself in any of these ways, the gains are much like those in the section "Should You Use A Study Group?" in Part 4—you develop leadership and teamwork skills that can only benefit you later in your career.

- *It's difficult to work and go to school.* There's an extra challenge and degree of difficulty for students who combine work and studies—as there is in the previous point for those who take on a role in addition to their studies. It's certainly clear these days that more students either want to or have to work as well as go to school. For many, a choice between the two is just not an option. But it's an undeniable reality that students' marks often suffer when they have a job. So be aware of the consequences if this situation applies to you, and know that you'll have to study even more effectively to get the top marks.

- *Your study skills are an asset as well as a tool.* While we've looked at study skills throughout this book as your best means of getting the top marks, as a tool, they are also a huge asset in your working life. It's a given that employers value employees who are skilled beyond merely the knowledge of their field of expertise—people who are able to lead, organize, structure and plan. These are the skills you develop from mastering our study strategies and they'll help you both as a student and as a valued employee.

THOUGHTS TO REMEMBER

I wish you all the best on your way to becoming a top student. The fact that you've chosen to attend school as a way of achieving your goals already shows that you're on the right track. And now that you're equipped with what you need to do the best job possible, you'll be able to arrive at your destination in good shape.

If it's true that "a journey of a thousand miles begins with one step," then you've taken one very important step by reading this book. Putting its thoughts and suggestions into practice is now up to you. But know that by doing so, you are now able to "go the distance" to your desired goal.

All the best!

NOTES

NOTES

NOTES

NOTES

PART 10

TEST TERMS

In the section "What to Do During Tests" in Part 7, we looked at a few examples of terms used in test and exam questions. Knowing exactly what these directions are calling for is critical to doing well in your answer. For example, if a test question asks you to "compare" two ideas and you "explain" the ideas without comparing them, your mark for that question will definitely be lower because you didn't do what the question wanted.

Here are explanations of the major terms that will show up in your test questions. Know what they mean and how to respond to them and you'll be well on your way to giving your best answer:

- *Analyze.* This term asks you to show how an idea or technique works. To do so, you usually have to break things down into their various parts, describe or explain each of the parts, and then show how the parts relate to each other.

- *Compare.* When you compare two or more ideas, techniques, or concepts, you're showing how they're alike in terms of their similarities or differences.

- *Contrast.* Contrasting two or more ideas, techniques, or

concepts means that you show only how they're different from each other.

- *Criticize or critique.* Here you're analyzing something and also making an evaluation or judgment about it. Start off by briefly showing how it works, then judge its value—"is it good or bad" or "is it right or wrong" are some examples.

- *Define.* This term calls for you to give a brief meaning of something, often with some specifics or details. You're trying to say "what it is."

- *Describe.* The purpose of description is to use your words to show "what it looks like." Get your reader to "see" in your writing the parts, details, or features of what you're describing.

- *Discuss.* A request to discuss something is a more general direction to debate its features or its values. This means that you might have to show how it works (analyze it) or how two things are the same or different (compare or contrast) by showing some positive or negative features. "Discuss" questions may or may not ask you to reach a conclusion.

- *Evaluate.* These are similar to "criticize" questions and also require your judgment, opinion, or viewpoint. Be specific by providing details and specific proof for your conclusion whether it's yours or that of someone else.

- *Explain.* "Explain" questions are a lot like ones that ask you to "describe" something. They want you to show why or how a process works or an idea develops. Again, make your answer clear by giving specifics.

- *Illustrate.* This is also similar to what you do in "explain" or "describe" type questions. In fact, to "illustrate" means to "draw" or "describe" something. Flesh out your answer with plenty of details, features, comparisons, facts, dates, and be as clear as possible.

- *Interpret.* Because this term literally means to "explain the meaning" of something, you're giving your viewpoint or version of it. For example, you can interpret the polling results of a political campaign in various ways, depending on the data involved. This is similar to "evaluate" so remember to back up your view with facts and details.

- *Justify.* What you're doing here is backing up your viewpoint with sufficient and significant reasons.

- *List.* Draw up a number of characteristics, features, qualities, or details that might be used to support a particular conclusion.

- *Outline.* This can be a point-form overview of an argument or the highlights of an idea.

- *Prove.* As with "justify," you're supporting your conclusion with relevant and specific main points. Since you can't simply make a claim without backing it up, the term "prove" instructs you to provide reasons for your point of view.

- *Relate or connect.* These terms are looking for the associations between ideas, concepts or facts. What you need to do is "join the dots" and make the connections clear.

- *State.* This direction wants you to give a specific explanation of something or reasons for something.

- *Summarize.* This is the "reader's digest" version of an idea, issue or concept. It wants a brief description or explanation giving only the most relevant points and omitting all unnecessary detail.

When you know what these terms mean and have some practice with them, you can go straight to the heart of any question and provide only what it requires. Too many times students try to do either too much in a question or they miss what the question asks for and give an answer that does something else. This shows the reader that these students didn't really understand the question and puts them at a disadvantage no matter how good their answer might have otherwise been.

SAMPLE TEST QUESTIONS

The following are some sample test questions that call for very specific responses. As a top student, you need to figure out quickly what each question needs you to do and to focus your answer in only those terms.

What students often don't realize is that test or exam questions call for only a specific and narrow answer. Even "general" or "broad-based" questions want you to give a just a few specific connections to give shape to a larger concept—they don't want the whole concept explained from A to Z.

The misjudgment that arises from students giving an answer that's "off base" is like the following example. Let's say that you call your dentist to ask about having your teeth cleaned, and the response you get is actually about what's involved in your getting a tooth filled. Both the question and the answer involve aspects of dentistry, but it's clear that the answer is not what the question called for. Similarly, if the dentist gave you a brief history of dentistry, that broad answer too would be off base.

So let's look at the following test questions and zero in as precisely as possible to identify the essence of what's called for. For our purposes, it's not really as important for us to answer each question as it is to figure out how to answer it.

Question 1
List the following groups of words into three columns according to their connotation: favorable, neutral, unfavorable.

    a) student, scholar, bookworm
    b) stubborn, firm, pig-headed
    c) counterfeit, replica, copy
    d) racy, obscene, blue
    e) unusual, bizarre, unique
    f) tolerant, flexible, wishy-washy
    g) caustic, penetrating, sharp
    h) reserved, aristocratic, snobbish
    i) buffoon, wit, comic
    j) svelte, skinny, thin

To answer this question quickly and effectively, it's important to know exactly what you need to do and in what order:

- If you've identified the words or phrases "list," "groups of words," "three columns," and connotation" as the important ones, you're off to a good start. The question is asking you to sort these sets of words into three columns.
- You also need to know that the "connotation" of these words—that is, the suggestive meanings they could possibly have—is the basis for clustering them.

- And you need to know that their meanings, or connotations, fall into the three categories of positive, neutral, and negative: or favorable, neutral, unfavorable.
- Now that you've figured out all of the important elements for giving the best answer, you're ready to use your dictionary or thesaurus to begin.
- Answers to a, b, and c: scholar/student/bookworm, firm/stubborn/pig-headed, replica/copy/counterfeit.

Question 2

Write a paragraph of 100 words on one of the following topics. Create a topic sentence that gives clear direction to the paragraph and provide reasons, examples, and details to support your point of view. Proofread and revise the paragraph before you hand it in.

1) Are older people always right?
2) Alcoholism is a family problem.
3) How to succeed as a student.
4) The rights of the physically disabled.
5) Lotteries.

Here are the things you should consider to focus your answer.

- Even before you look at the question, don't be fooled by the brevity of the answer—shorter answers are usually more difficult to write than longer ones. They require you to focus your response extremely clearly rather than "pad" your answer or ramble. You need to choose every word and idea with precision.

- Identify the role of each of the three sentences in the question. Sentence 1 gives you the "big picture" of the task and the topic choices while Sentence 3 addresses the "follow up" requirements of checking and revision. You'll need to give an amount of time to each of these, of course, but your main focus is on Sentence 2.

- A breakdown of Sentence 2 calls for you to write a clear "topic sentence" or viewpoint of the topic; then to back it up with "reasons, examples and details."

- Going back to Sentence 1, you see that you have to choose one of the 5 topics. Be aware that they're not all the same: for instance, Topic 1 asks for you to agree or disagree while Topic

2 is set up as a statement of fact. If your answer were to disagree with Topic 2, your answer would already be missing the point of the question before you even started to write it. Note that Topic 5 doesn't even come with a point of view, so it's essential that you come up with one—don't take this as a sign that it's acceptable to just ramble on about the topic.

- Once you pick your topic, you need to divide your time carefully. If you have an hour to write, you'd give the first 15-20 minutes to think out your answer and create an outline, and about 10 minutes at the end to go over it. That would leave you with 30-35 minutes to actually write it out. Giving more time at the beginning to structure your answer carefully means that you won't need all that much time for writing.

Question 3

Analyze the differences between these two paragraphs. Make your critique as specific as possible.

1) Our evaluation shows that the Titan processor offers many of the features you need, but at 20% higher cost compared to the ZX2 and the Speedwriter, both of which have similar features. The ultra high speed of the Titan is also an advantage, although there is some doubt whether you would use the extra speed enough to warrant the additional cost. The moderate speed of the ZX2 offers a reasonable alternative and still ensures the purchase would be within the budget you established in your letter of March 11. The Speedwriter has a similar speed and price, but has a six-month delivery delay.

2) The ZX2 processor has the best combination of features and price. It is not the fastest processor we evaluated, but it offers similar features to both the Titan and the Speedwriter and it falls within the budget price you established in your letter of March 11. The Titan has a higher speed, which we doubt you would use sufficiently to warrant its 20% higher cost. The Speedwriter is the same price as the ZX2, but has a six-month delivery date.

- At first glance, there might not seem to be much to go on in the question's instructions. But when you look closely, the word "analyze" is a big one—requiring you to break down each paragraph into parts, and then explaining and relating those parts.

150

- The word "differences" clearly points to your need to highlight the contrasts or differences between the paragraphs.

- The result of your contrast of the strengths and weaknesses of the paragraphs then has to lead you to a "critique" of them in an evaluation or judgment as to which is better.

- Finally, you need to support your judgment with specific points.

- Obviously, in order to answer the question well, you need to look for things like writing style, sentence structure, tone, and structure of argument. An analysis of these features would lead you to conclude that Paragraph 2 is superior to Paragraph 1.

- This example shows that even though the instructions appear to be minimal, you still need to read closely to determine accurately the intent of the question. Otherwise, there remains the strong possibility that you might think that it's an "anything goes" situation and miss the purpose of the question.

Question 4

Read the attached poem and respond to the following 3 questions:

1) Briefly explain what happens in each stanza. Identify the meanings of key words. Be sure to refer to all the important parts of the work.
2) What comparisons or contrasts are there? Identify any similarities or contrasts among the stanzas. For example, is the person in the poem young at the beginning and old at the end? Is the person weak at the beginning but stronger or wiser at the end? Is the setting wild or chaotic at the start and peaceful at the end?
3) Explain the controlling idea. Summarize the theme and show how it develops throughout.

- I didn't include the poem because we just need to look at the question.

- Unlike the directions in the previous question, these are significantly more detailed and thorough.

- It's important to notice that there are sets and sub-sets to the overall question. The overall question itself is divided into three sets (parts 1-3) and each of these sets is further divided into subsets (more detailed questions).

- A key thing you should realize here is that this kind of detailed question means that you need to be very careful to address each and every part of the question—major and minor. This isn't an invitation for you to "pick and choose" parts of the question that you prefer while leaving other parts out. You need to answer everything.

- Although you need to address all aspects of the question, there's no need to do so equally. A major part requires more thought and detail that a minor part does, so divide your time and attention accordingly.

- If you have one hour to respond, that means your first order of business is to allocate 20 minutes to each of the 3 parts. If you decide that the parts are roughly the same in terms of the substance and detail required by each part, then that's a reasonable time allocation.

- Identify whether the parts can be answered in the numerical order in which they appear, or whether another order would be better. (Answering these in the order that they appear is preferable).

- See if you can detect a pattern of development. For example, when you look at what each of the parts asks for, you see that Part 1 calls simply calls for brief "explanations" and descriptions of "meanings"; Part 2 becomes more complex by looking for comparisons and contrasts; and Part 3 contains the biggest ideas and requirements by wanting you to relate the main idea and show its pattern of expression throughout. This kind of movement from "small" to "large," from "simple" to "complex," shows that the structure of the question is moving from micro to macro ideas.

It's important to consider all of the elements in these questions before rushing off to write just any kind of answer. The more your answers address all of these concerns—and only these concerns—the higher mark they'll get.

Answers that try to include everything about the topic miss the specifics of what these questions call for and won't get top marks. They "miss the target" by doing too much that isn't asked for while ignoring the details that are required.

NOTES

154

NOTES

NOTES

156

NOTES

NOTES